BRITAIN
IN OLD PHOTOGRAPHS

KIRKCALDY & EAST FIFE

BRUCE DURIE

SUTTON PUBLISHING

Sutton Publishing Limited
Phoenix Mill · Thrupp · Stroud
Gloucestershire · GL5 2BU

First published 2002

Title page photograph courtesy of Don Swanson.

British Library Cataloguing in Publication Data
A catalogue record for this book is available from the
British Library.

ISBN 0-7509-2829-8

Typeset in 10.5/13.5 Photina.
Typesetting and origination by
Sutton Publishing Limited.
Printed and bound in England by
J.H. Haynes & Co. Ltd, Sparkford.

The working horses, like that shown on the previous page, are gone from Fife's towns. More common are their smaller cousins at children's farms, visitor attractions and, as here, the Beveridge Park in Kirkcaldy. But these will also disappear as their attraction wanes and concern over animal welfare increases. *(DS)*

CONTENTS

Road and rail links put Fife firmly on the map as a destination in its own right as well as a route for transport heading north or south. This postcard depicts the Tay Bridge from North Fife, before the building of the parallel road bridge. *(BD)*

Abbotshall Church, shown here around 1900, but dating from 1788, commemorates in its name the siting of the property gifted to the Abbot of Dunfermline in 1075 so his monks could keep an eye on the Celtic Christians along the road. Queen Margaret was keen to impress Roman Catholicism on her subjects and to suppress the existing churches. Abbotshall was a separate parish until it was integrated into Kirkcaldy and Dysart, along with part of Kinghorn parish, in 1901. The best known inhabitant of the church's cemetery is the child prodigy Pet Marjorie, favourite of Sir Walter Scott, who was buried here after her death in 1811 aged eight. Bennochy Mill (see page 81) can be seen on the right. *(JS)*

The County Buildings (now called the Sheriff Court) were built in 1894 to accommodate the needs of the County Council. The Sheriff Clerk conducted all legal business from here. Constructed in the Scottish Baronial style, for years it formed one of three sides of an impressive civic square with the post office opposite and the Town House between (see page 67). A recent extension has increased its utility but not its attractiveness. *(JS)*

THE KINGDOM OF FIFE
THE FIRST 8,000 YEARS

'Fife's got everything' is the proud boast of the Fifers and they can be forgiven for occasionally portraying their Kingdom as a miniature, east-coast Scottish California. Fife possesses a unique mixture of history and living culture, industry and rural economy, an unrivalled combination of seashore, hills, fields, forests, small villages and large townscapes, with a strong sense of self and an outward-looking approach. Fife is the home of golf, linoleum and Adam Smith, with the world's best haggis, Britain's best chip shop and Scotland's best pub, seat of an ancient capital and burial place of kings, host to Europe's oldest and largest annual funfair and to Britain's best aquarium, centre of Silicon Glen and motherland to poets, novelists and musicians. Excessive bounty, it seems. And how has all this come to bless one small corner of a small country? The answer is in the geography. Fife is conveniently bordered by the Firth of Forth to the south and the Firth of Tay to the north. These estuaries, and the rivers which feed them, have proved their strategic worth over the centuries. The Romans never made much headway beyond the Tay apart from a brief skirmish and their only real victory in Scotland – at Mons Graupius (probably Bennachie in Angus). They obviously thought better of trying to subjugate the Picts of *Fib* and built the third of their great barriers, the Antonine wall, to fence off the area beyond the Forth and Clyde so they could ignore it. Later, William Wallace and King Robert Bruce successfully prevented English incursions across the Forth.

The Kingdom of Fife – and that name alone suggests what the natives think of it – makes the best of its physical identity by remaining resolutely unitary, more or less untouched by the vicissitudes of boundary changes which have swept away or simply ignored the likes of Rutland, Roxburghshire and the Yorkshire Ridings. In contrast to most other parts of the UK, the council, health board, local enterprise company, tourist board, European structural funding areas, chamber of commerce and parliamentary seats all have the same footprint. The Scottish Enterprise Network would have it otherwise, in a typical attempt to complicate things in order to simplify, so that north Fife would be subject to Dundee and south Fife feu'd to Edinburgh. This would assuredly disrupt the close partnership which has been a characteristic of Fife for more than two millennia.

When the glaciers retreated after the last ice age they left a fertile, coastal, east-facing area, cut off as the land rose and the North Sea formed. Whatever Mesolithic peoples were pushed westwards by the rising melt-water sea, some settled in Morton and Tentsmuir, near present-day St Andrews, around 6000BC – possibly the oldest human settlement in Scotland. We know little of them except that they lived off easily collected mussels, crabs, limpets and other marine life, supplemented by the nuts, berries, roots and leafy plants

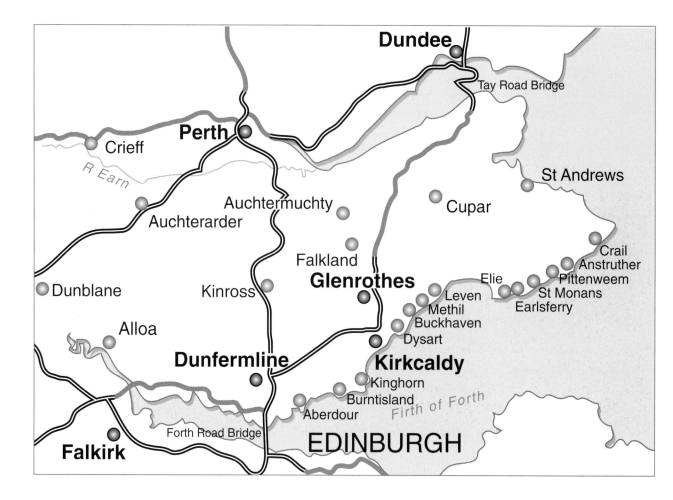

which quickly grew inland, plus the occasional unlucky animal. The entire population of Scotland was probably only a few hundred and Fife maybe a dozen or two. Eight millennia later, Fife is still dependent on its fishing and its agriculture, and while most of the deer are in farms and visitor centres, they still contribute to the local economy.

In Neolithic times and through the long Bronze Age, the population steadily grew. Around 500–400BC the Gaelic-speaking Celts swept into Scotland from the continent and brought with them the Iron Age. They established themselves first on the shores of the River Tay and covered the hills of North Fife and Perthshire with forts, many still visible.

Some 800 years later, the early Christian missionaries arrived. One of them, St Rule, a monk from Patras in western Greece, brought relics of St Andrew – an arm bone, a knee-cap, a tooth and three fingers from the right hand. As the local Pictish king went to meet the stranger and his retinue, a great white cross appeared across blue sky. This eventually became the national flag of Scotland (and of St Rule when he was martyred).

In the aftermath of the Norman invasion in 1066 Margaret arrived, an English princess brought up in safety in Hungary. Blown off course, her ship landed near Dunfermline and she became the queen of Malcolm Canmore within a few months. Dunfermline was then the capital of Scotland. After her death a shrine was erected in her memory and later her son King David built the magnificent Benedictine Dunfermline Abbey. The ashes of all of Margaret but her head are still there. She was later canonised.

The fertile Howe of Fife has long provided for many small settlements. These early postcards show the flat plain from Cupar (above) and the village of Strathmiglo (below) sheltered by the hills. *(BD)*

It was in Fife that Alexander III plunged to his death (at Kinghorn in 1285 or 1286, see page 24), setting off a dynastic struggle that lasted thirty years. Fife was where Macduff led his 1054 revolt against Macbeth; where King Robert Bruce's parents courted in the 1270s; where Mary of Lorraine landed (Balcomie); where Sir Henry Wood smashed Henry VIII's navy (off Crail near the May Isle in 1546); where Andrew Selkirk, alias Robinson Crusoe, sailed from (Largo, page 112); where the Spanish survivors of the Armada arrived (Anstruther); where Cardinal Beaton was slung into an unknown grave (Kilrenny in 1546); where James V crossed the Dreel Burn on the back of a peasant woman (Anstruther, page 122); where linoleum was made and *The Wealth of Nations* written (Kirkcaldy); and where Andrew Carnegie, the world's richest man at the turn of the twentieth century, spread much of his benefice (Dunfermline).

In the middle ages the Earls of Fife had the hereditary right to crown the Scottish king and to lead his armies into battle. Fife was also the home of Scotland's largest and leading church, the cathedral at St Andrews. St Andrews University was founded in 1411. Fife also had royal palaces: Falkland, unparalleled for its grand Renaissance style, was the favourite of Scottish monarchs for 200 years. It has the oldest real (or royal) tennis court in Scotland, built for James V in 1539 and still in use. And of course Fife has been the home of golf for 500 years.

The Fife coast's open aspect and good natural harbours made it a natural sea-faring area, but also a target for piracy and invasion. Along the coast are many defences and observation points guarding the seaways to Edinburgh and Leith across the Forth, and out to the North Sea, as here at Ravenscraig (see page 83). *(BD)*

The magnificent Dunfermline Abbey, next to Malcolm Canmore's palace, was built in memory of the eleventh-century Queen Margaret, Malcolm's wife and a civilising influence on the Fifers. She died in Edinburgh Castle on 16 November 1093 and was buried before the Altar of the Holy Cross in the church she had founded in Dunfermline. When she was canonised in 1250 her body was translated from its original burial site inside Dunfermline Abbey to the east end of the abbey church where it could be venerated by pilgrims. Her skull was encased in a reliquary – a silver and gold likeness adorned with pearls, chains and precious stones – and her hair could be viewed through a crystal on the breast of the figure. Reputedly, fearing Protestant vandalism during the turbulent years of the Scottish Reformation and following the Treaty of Berwick between Elizabeth I and the reformers, Abbot George Durie took the head-shrine to his castle at Craigluscar or to Rossend (see page 19) in 1560. He died the next year. In 1597 the shrine was handed to the Jesuits and then transported by one of them, John Robie, to Antwerp. Eventually it found its way to France but disappeared during the French Revolution in 1789. *(DS)*

Fife has long been a major ecclesiastical centre. The ruins of St Andrews Cathedral, shown in this 1903 postcard, were the site of Scotland's premier church for centuries. The earliest clerics to live in St Andrews were the Celtic speaking Culdees (from *céli dé*, companions of God) an informal grouping of non-celibate clergymen established in the early part of the ninth century. *(BD)*

THORNTON DRAMA

1915.

THORNTON

1915

DD1 1DD

k

They made their own amusement in those days! This postcard commemorates the antics of the Thornton Dramatic Club in 1915, although the title of the actual performance is not detailed. *(BD)*

The monks who settled and started to mine the strange, black, combustible rock began a coal industry that fuelled other businesses – salt-panning, pottery, glass-making, engineering, distilling, shipbuilding. The industry flourished until the general mining collapse of the 1960s and '70s, but some mining continues at Longannet and elsewhere.

Fife was equally famed for its rich merchants and thriving European trade. All along the East Neuk were royal burghs and burghs of barony that were home to merchant seamen, fishermen and salty sea-dogs who fought the English pirates. The fishing industry survives precariously at Pittenweem, and the picturesque villages with stately homes and castles nearby are major tourist attractions. The rivers and the excellent harbours provided for the East Neuk's fishing and Kirkcaldy's whaling and supported Fife's burgeoning trade with England, northern Europe and further afield. Ships left laden with coal, fish, salt, whisky and finished products, and came back with raw materials, immigrant peoples and the red roof tiles that give east Fife houses a Dutch look to this day.

When the Forth–Clyde canal was built, the route to the west was opened up. The cereals and soft fruits grown in the flat, alluvial plain of the Howe of Fife made this one of the largest produce-growing areas in Britain by the 1900s. Fife's fields were the source of wheat for bread, barley for brewing and distilling, and oats for Scott's porridge, itself a great cultural icon.

Today, Fife is home to some 350,000 souls and the number is steadily increasing as Edinburgh house prices drive commuters to discover the pleasures of living 30 minutes or less away by rail or road over one of the two Forth bridges. Dundee is equally accessible via two Tay bridges. The central belt, Glasgow and the west can be reached readily via the M90, as can Perth and the north up the A9.

South and west Fife are dominated by large urban areas and an industrial economy – Dunfermline, Inverkeithing and the ex-coal towns of Cowdenbeath and Lochgelly. Central and north Fife has the old agricultural centre of Cupar, the new town of Glenrothes and the ancient ecclesiastical, university and golfing burgh of St Andrews. The east is mainly agricultural with idyllic small fishing villages which are a haven for tourists and artists alike but with major industrial or post-industrial centres at Kirkcaldy and Levenmouth.

Fife, like many other parts of Scotland and the UK, has weathered significant, deep-rooted changes in its economic base over the past century and even more so since 1945. Mining, textiles, pottery and heavy engineering have had to give way to a mixture of electronics, precision engineering, tourism and a large retail/service sector. High streets are dying in the famine imposed by industrial estates, business complexes and out-of-town retail parks. The workforce demographics have changed, leaving significant unemployment and retraining problems. On the other hand, people are well-housed and generally not starving. One thing is for sure – Fifers don't take a problem lying down and usually spring back quickly. They say 'it takes a long spoon to sup with a Fifer'. The Fifer will even sell you the spoon.

Author's note: This book necessarily deals mostly with Fife's largest and major town, Kirkcaldy, and the changes it has seen during the last, remarkable century, written by someone who watched half of it happen. But it also takes a journey up the east coast from Aberdour to Crail and tries to set the present in the context of the past. It could have been a larger book or a different book. And there will be other books.

1

Aberdour, Burntisland & Kinghorn

Inchcolm Abbey, sometimes called 'the Iona of the East', sits on a small island off Aberdour. It was founded by King Alexander I who found a safe haven there during a storm in 1123, courtesy of a hermit who welcomed the king into his home. In thanks for his deliverance, Alexander endowed a priory in honour of St Columba. Even by 1904 when this picture was taken most of the priory – the earliest part of the building – was in ruins, although the later Chapter House and Scriptorium remain. Trips to the island run during the summer months from South Queensferry (under the Forth Bridge) and other ports. The postcard contains a small mystery – what are those men doing on the tower roof?

Aberdour

Although Aberdour sits small, quiet and secluded on the Fife coast, it is only 20 miles from Edinburgh and 3 miles from the busy M90 motorway. Aberdour (literally, 'Mouth of the Water') has two high-quality beaches – the Silver Sands has European Union 'Blue Flag' status. The twelfth-century St Fillan's Church and thirteenth-century castle are witness to its antiquity. A stone pier built in the 1700s to allow larger vessels access to the natural harbour, formed by the Dour Burn and Hawkcraig Point, brought prosperity to the village. Marine trade was largely superseded by the railway when Aberdour station opened in 1890. The village was popular with Victorian paddle-steamer day-trippers from Edinburgh. Hawkcraig Point was used as a Royal Navy Base for developing and testing underwater acoustic detection equipment during the First World War and in both world wars the fleet stationed in the Forth was serviced and maintained in Aberdour. The railway station became passenger-only in the 1940s. However, it routinely wins 'best kept railway station' competitions. The village is now mainly a tourist resort and commuting base for Edinburgh, Dundee and Glasgow.

The Woodside Hotel, previously known as Greig's Hotel, was built in 1873 by the Greig brothers of Inverkeithing, whose great-grandfather had helped to found the Imperial Russian Navy. The smaller picture shows the elaborate ceiling, bought in 1926 from the steamship *Oronted* which had sailed between Britain and Australia. The building, listed as being of architectural interest, had a complete refurbishment in 1995 following a devastating fire. *(Stewart Dykes)*

The Aberdour Festival was started in 1984 by a willing band of volunteers. The idea was to involve the whole community in four summer days of social, cultural and sporting activities. Now it runs for eight days at the beginning of August. The festival marquee is situated beside the famous Silver Sands, a beautiful stretch of sandy beach regularly commended for its cleanliness. This picture shows festival activities in and around Aberdour Castle.

Aberdour Castle was once the property of Thomas Randolph who fought alongside Robert Bruce at Bannockburn. It passed to the Douglas family in 1342 and thence to James Douglas who became Lord Aberdour and Earl Morton in 1458. After three generations the castle passed by marriage to Sir George Douglas, later 4th Earl of Morton, Regent of Scotland during Queen Mary's minority and a leading plotter in the murder of her husband Lord Darnley. For this he was executed in 1581. His daughter-in-law Jean Lyon, by then widowed, married Lord Spynie. William, the 6th Earl, inherited title and castle in 1607 after Spynie's death. He reconstructed much of it and added more, including the east wing and the walled garden. The castle was badly damaged by fire in 1688 (not 1715 during an occupation by dragoons as is often said). In 1690 the 10th Earl had plans drawn for the rebuilding, but this never took place. It was abandoned in favour of Cuttlehill House (page 16) in 1725. Now held by Historic Scotland and open to the public from April to September, the castle has large gardens, a restored first-floor gallery and an unusual beehive-shaped dovecot. *(DS)*

When the Mortons gave up Aberdour Castle in 1725 they built Cuttlehill, now Aberdour House. After Robert Watson died in 1791, parts of the building were used as a barracks, a school, a masonic hall, a piggery and a cowshed. It was still a family home until the 1920s when it was taken into state ownership and it is now divided into a number of flats. *(BD)*

Burntisland

Burntisland – it's not an island and it isn't burnt. There is a fair amount of historical flummery around the name Burntisland, with stories of Romans burning native cottages and the like. But in 1506 the monks of Dunfermline knew it as Byrtiland, and the second burgh charter of 1585 uses the same name. In 1540 it is recorded as Bert iland – the name is probably of Scandinavian origin as it would have been a known safe harbour for Danes. A competing theory has the name derived from the Old British Bryn Telin, meaning 'half carcase hill' since the Binn is partly blown outwards by volcanic eruption. The word Binn itself may be a corruption or misreading of Bryn. There is also the Scots word 'bruntlin' (burnt moor) or it may derive from Brunt's Land (like Bruntsfield in Edinburgh). Certainly there have been Brands in the town for centuries.

A 4,000-year-old Pictish fort sits on the highest point of the Binn Hill and a cinerary urn of that period was found in 1866 during the building of Binn House (since demolished). The Roman commander Agricola camped on nearby Dunearn Hill, making use of Burntisland's natural harbour. Rossend Castle (page 19) was built in 1119, King David I granted lands for a church to the Abbots of Dunfermline at Kirkton in 1130, and the town, then known as Wester Kinghorn, grew up around it. The Bishop of St Andrews consecrated the church in 1243.

Recognising the value of Burntisland's harbour as a naval port, James V granted a charter to form a royal burgh in 1541, confirmed by James VI in 1586. Burntisland became the second most important port on the Forth after Leith, and shipbuilding was a major industry in Burntisland for the next four centuries.

The Royal Burgh of Burntisland sits on the south coast of Fife, 6 miles from Kirkcaldy and looking across to Edinburgh. The town crest bears the mottos 'Portus Gratiae' (Safe Harbour) and 'Colles Praesidio Dedit Deus' (God Gave the Hills for Protection), referring to the town's maritime history and the extinct volcano of Binn Hill behind the town. This 1960s picture shows the open-air swimming pool, now long gone (see page 20) and the view across to Edinburgh. *(Dunfermline Press Group)*

St Columba's church, started in 1592 and completed in 1595, has a Dutch look, following the fashion of the Reformation, with a central pulpit to hammer home the principle of equality in the eyes of God. It has several remarkable features including guild seats, marked pews for the gentry and a sailors' loft from which men could leave quietly during a service if the tides or winds were right for sailing. The church, said to be the first built after the Reformation, hosted the General Assembly in 1601, where King James VI (then staying at Rossend Castle) agreed to a new translation of the Bible – the Authorised or King James Version. An accident of history meant it appeared in vernacular English as opposed to Scots. The church was recently renovated inside after a partial roof collapse. (NB)

Opposite: Rossend Castle gateway, *c.* 1900, and the castle today. The gateway has since been cleared of its attractive foliage. Built in 1119 and extended in 1382 and 1563, Rossend Castle overlooks the Firth of Forth at the western end of Burntisland. It was visited by many of the kings and queens of Scotland including Mary Queen of Scots in 1563. A French poet, Chastellard, was discovered hiding in her bedchamber, for which he was executed at St Andrews (this was his second offence; the first occurred in Holyrood). Rossend is said to have been the hiding place of the relics of Queen Margaret, taken there by George Durie, Abbot of Dunfermline, before they were sent to Europe for safe keeping. The castle was the residence of the Duries until the Reformation and later of Sir Alexander Gibson, who took the judicial title Lord Durie. Rossend Castle has been restored to its former glory by a firm of architects and is currently used as the firm's main offices *(opposite above, BD; opposite below, NB)*.

The sweep of Burntisland's excellent beach, the wide, shallow, sandy bay – popular for watersports – and the natural harbour beyond can be seen in this modern photograph. The famous outdoor swimming pool is gone (see page 17), replaced by The Beacon leisure centre with a heated indoor pool, water flumes and the rest. French ships and troops were blockaded in the town by the English in 1560 and the port was a muster area during the threat of the Spanish Armada in 1588. But most famously of all, Charles I, on his only tour of Scotland, lost a huge treasure and other possessions when the ferry *The Blessing of Burntisland* sank crossing the Forth. The vessel has now been found. In 1651 Cromwell's warships bombarded the town and English troops took it, remaining in garrison until 1660. In 1667 Dutch warships attacked, launching almost 500 cannonballs in protest against the privateering activities of the local ships acting under Letters of Marque. At the peak of the herring fishing in about 1800 nearly 500 boats would offload in the harbour for the half-dozen or more curing factories. The coal industry and the railway maintained the town's prosperity in the Victorian era. The railway station was built in 1847 and the world's first rail ferry started here in 1850, but the building of the Forth Bridge in 1890 rendered it unnecessary. The area was still important as a service yard for trains – the North British Railway Company built and maintained engines and carriages for many years. In 1878 James 'Paraffin' Young started a shale-oil business on the Binn Hill and founded a village to accommodate his workforce.

During the First World War the British Aluminium Company built a plant which was serviced by the railway and docks. In 1984 after the merger of British Aluminium with the Canadian firm Alcan a new plant was opened. Bauxite ore is still imported, the dust giving the access roads a distinctive red colour. Burntisland was also a centre for brewing and distilling, which continued until 1916, and for shipbuilding from 1918 to 1968. The shipyard had an international reputation between 1919 and 1969, and today builds rig modules for the offshore oil industry. But its greatest claim to fame was in 1938 when the football team Burntisland Shipyard, founded in the 1920s, almost held Celtic to a draw in the Scottish Cup. With 20 minutes to go the 'Shippie' were level 3–3 then Celtic were awarded a penalty and went on to win 8–3. *(NB)*

Somerville Square has had several names – Midgait, Back Street and Quality Street (a reference to the fact that the 'quality' lived there). Most of the houses in the picture above were demolished or renovated in recent years. Those on the left were buildings of historical significance. The nearest, Mary Somerville's house (built in 1596 and acquired by Captain George Fairfax, father of Mary Somerville, in 1789) proved to have a secret stairway and a painted ceiling of interest to the Historic Building Commission, who funded the restoration. And who was Mary Somerville? Possibly Britain's first female scientist. Somerville College, Oxford, is named after her. Her first published book, *The Mechanism of the Heavens* (1831), sold over 700 copies at Cambridge University alone. She was granted a royal pension of £300 a year to continue her scientific works and later published *The Connection of the Physical Sciences*, *Physical Geography* and *Molecular and Microscopic Science*. (NB)

Next door to Mary Somerville's House (now a masonic lodge) was the home of James Robertson, who became the Civil Governor of New York in 1782. Further along is Watson's Mortification, four houses once occupied free of charge by a schoolmaster and three widows. The houses on the left of Somerville Square were modernised by the town council in the late 1950s. *(NB)*

Brought up in Burntisland, rock star and Nazareth drummer Darrell Sweet (1947–99) died of a heart attack while on tour in New Albany, Indiana. In 2001 a memorial plaque was erected in the stadium where he collapsed. Darrell's sister, Melanie Cameron, lives in Burntisland and went to America with their mother, Margaret Casey, to see the plaque installed. The photograph is printed here courtesy of Brian Baxter who was instrumental in establishing Darrell's memorial. From left to right are Maggie Hollis, Melanie Cameron, Margaret Casey and Brian Baxter. *(BB)*

Sadly, the town has fallen from its state of grace as a favoured holiday resort and is now dominated by ugly industrial buildings (below) and empty or derelict buildings such as the cinema in the High Street (above). *(ND)*

Kinghorn

Formerly a ferry port with thriving shipbuilding and spinning industries, Kinghorn is now better known as a holiday centre. Pettycur had a battery of Royal Engineers in residence at the turn of the twentieth century as part of a scheme to improve the defences of the Forth, along with three batteries on Inchkeith to provide cross-fire over the deep channel on the Fife side of the estuary. The harbour was also home to a thriving ferry which served the coach trade north and south, linking with Newhaven. For many years milestones in Fife recorded the distance to Pettycur. The coming of the railway transferred the ferryports to Burntisland on the north and Granton on the Edinburgh side.

Between Burntisland and Kinghorn is the monument to Alexander III, last of Scotland's Celtic kings, who lived and ruled in the second half of the thirteenth century. Alexander was riding to Dunfermline one stormy night in 1286 to visit his new bride when his horse slipped and he fell to his death. When the memorial was built in 1886 it was placed not at the actual site of Alexander's plunge, but further along where the view across the Forth was more scenic. It was the inspiration of Thomas Nelson, the Edinburgh publisher, and was designed by the elegantly named Mr Hippolyte J. Blanc. (BD)

The elegant Kinghorn Town Building has been left to rot despite the efforts of the local Heritage Trust. *(ND)*

AFTER successfully carrying on business of Glue Manufacturers for a century in Kinghorn, the Firm have found it necessary, by the exigencies of trade, to remove to more extensive works, which have been erected at CURRIE, near Edinburgh, specially built for the Manufacturing of

GLUES & GELATINES

Customers, Manufacturers, and Trades generally can remain confident that the prestige of the firm will be upheld.

J. D. & S. purpose to extend their manufactures and produce the various grades required to supply the demands of the market.

Sold in Cake, Size, Powder.

Made up in Different Sized Packages.

WHOLESALE TRADE Supplied. —— Ask for Prices.

New Address:

Kinghorn Glue & Gelatine Works,

CURRIE, N.B.

A royal burgh since 1170, Kinghorn's former castle was frequently visited by the Scottish court. The earldom of Strathmore and Kinghorne is held by the present Queen Mother's family. Shipbuilding and engineering were represented by Scott & Co. at the eastern end of the town and at the west end the glue works dominated the beach when this photograph was taken in about 1900. Kinghorn was long the centre of Scotland's renowned glue-making industry – the trade name of Scotch Tape bears witness to this. John Darney started manufacture at the end of the eighteenth century in a works which existed up to the 1900s, bringing the new techniques of chemistry and industrial engineering to bear on a craft still practised using medieval methods. The firm later moved to Currie, near Edinburgh as the advert opposite shows. *(JS)*

Much the same view as that above but in more recent times, this picture shows the addition of tourist facilities such as the shelter and the ice-cream shop. *(KYL)*

Pettycur Bay is still a popular resort with holiday homes and caravans near the harbour (above) and clustered between the Binn Hill and Kinghorn (below). *(ND)*

2
Kirkcaldy

Kirkcaldy High Street before the tramways were built in 1903. *(DS)*

Some say the Deil's deid an' buriet in Kirkcaldy
The Deil's aye kind tae his ain
A man should hae as muckle o' the Dei in him as keep the Deil oot
He maun hae a lang spne that sups wi' the Deil

Kirkcaldy is an ancient town. The earliest known record of its existence dates from the Battle of Raith in AD596 when Aedan mac Gabrain, overking of Dalriada, led a coalition of local Picts, Scots from the west and Britons from further south in Gododdin (now Lothian) and fought off the invading Angles. The name 'Raith' is a reference to a *rath* or hill-fort and the hill-top Raith Estate survives to this day. The name is also preserved in the local football team, Raith Rovers, which justifiably entered into legend when an English football commentator displayed his ignorance of Scottish geography by proclaiming, after the team's victory, 'They'll be dancing in the streets of Raith tonight.' More likely they were dancing in the Raith Ballroom.

The name Kirkcaldy has four proposed origins. One is Caer Calad Dun, or fort on the hill. Another is Caer Caledonii, fort of the Caledoni, a local tribe. The third is from Calaten (the sons of Calaten were famous magicians). And the fourth means Kirk of the Culdees, the Columban order prevalent in early Scotland, but later suppressed by the Abbot of Dunfermline after St Margaret promoted Roman Catholicism. The Abbot built an outpost near the town (now Abbotshall) from which to watch these dangerous heretics. Whichever derivation is correct, when the town was gifted to Dunfermline Abbey in 1075 it was referred to as Kirkcaladunt. The theories linking the town's name to a hill fort and a church both ring true, the Kirk being a reference to the one founded by St Bryce (also known as Brisse, Bricius or Britius, meaning 'the Briton'), who became Bishop of Tours in AD397 and travelled to Scotland with St Ninian. It is unclear whether Bryce himself ever visited Kirkcaldy, but Ninian's chapel at Bogie Farm is remembered in the name of nearby Chapel Village, and Abden House, between Kirkcaldy and Kinghorn, takes it name from him as the Ab (abbot).

The Old Kirk's siting in Kirk Wynd (see page 80) on a hill overlooking the High Street would have put it in a commanding position in the medieval town centre. It is possible that it was built on a Culdee church site. Ninian, Bryce and the other missionaries of the fifth century were not pioneers, but bishops visiting and consolidating existing converts and ordaining new clerics, so there may have been a Culdee church on the site already. After his death in 444 Bryce was commemorated at Marmoutier, a religious house near Tours. French monks came to Canterbury in the twelfth century, and monks from Canterbury were invited to Dunfermline. This was also a time when Norman families settled in Fife. Possibly some of them came from Marmoutier and wanted to perpetuate the memory of their patron saint in the new church.

When King Malcolm III provided the foundation charter for Dunfermline church (now the abbey) in 1075, the Shire of Kirkcaladinit was also bestowed and its incomes used to fund the building work. In 1240 the Bishop of St Andrews, David de Bernham, bestowed the Church of Kirkcaldy on the Abbey of Dunfermline, which had to provide its vicars. A document in the National Library of Paris records the consecration of the church of Kirkcaldy on 21 March 1244 and its dedication to St Patrick and St Brisse (St Bryce). (It may be that an early version of the Links Market was held near St Patrick's Day 17 March – which would have been a holiday and a market.) It stayed under the control of the Dunfermline Abbey until 1450, when the burgh, rents, harbour and petty customs were ceded to the burgh magistrates. After the Reformation, the vicar of the Old Kirk was retired, and George Scott, brother of Thomas Scott, Laird of Abbotshall, became the first Protestant minister there.

Kirkcaldy is also known as 'The Lang Toun' because of its long seafront – 4 miles under the current boundaries – and came to be that way when a series of villages and

Nothing exemplifies Kirkcaldy's last 100 years as much as the sight of old industrial buildings brought to new and previously unthought-of uses. The West Mill, once a bustling factory, dates from the 1850s when Thomas Renton opened a roperie, making cables for ships including the *Queen Mary*. The West Mill also made the famous Post Office parcel twine.

Closing in 1973, the mill stood empty for many years but then became a combined conference centre, business facility and accommodation-plus-jobs project for the homeless.

The picture at the top shows the building as it stood empty *(DS)*; the middle photograph illustrates the use made of the existing structure when it was re-roofed *(DS)*; and the bottom picture is The Forum, as West Mill is now known. *(BD)*

burghs running from west to east were linked together – Invertiel, Bridgeton, the burgh of Linktown, the burgh of Kirkcaldy, the burgh of Pathhead, Sinclairtown, Gallatown, part of the Raith Estate, and more recently, the burgh of Dysart. Daniel Defoe described Kirkcaldy as 'one street, one mile long'.

The town grew up around its harbour near the mouth of the East Burn, although it gradually extended along the shore to the West Burn or Tiel but never went more than two furlongs inland at this time. By 1584 stronger walls and gates were being built and jealously guarded. Over a hundred ships are thought to have been anchored in the harbour by the early 1600s, but Kirkcaldy's shipping suffered heavy losses during the Civil Wars when Cromwell occupied the town. Kirkcaldy was formally chartered as a royal burgh in 1644, confirmed by Charles II in 1661. It grew to be the largest town in Fife and was the administrative centre of the county and – after local government reorganisation – of Kirkcaldy District from 1975 to 1996 when the region disappeared and the district with it.

Scotland as a whole suffered from swingeing 'navigation laws' in the seventeenth century which denied trade with North America. This hit Glasgow and the west harder than Fife, with its ready view to northern Europe. Trade gradually picked up again, especially as the weaving and spinning industries grew in the 1700s. Linen became increasingly important from the mid-1730s and machinery for flax spinning was introduced in the last decade of the eighteenth century. The 1800s saw the development of the textile and coalmining industries. A floor-cloth factory opened in 1847 and linoleum was first made in 1876. The fortunes generated by this and related industries gave the town many of its municipal amenities and prestige buildings such as Beveridges, Nairns and Oswalds. Other factory owners fell over each other to prove their relative philanthropy. The economic expansion brought the development of the High Street as a retail area and new parallel streets further away from the shore emphasised Kirkcaldy's decreasing reliance on harbour trade.

To this day the main manufacturing concern is floor coverings, the most famous of which – linoleum – is again being produced after a brief cessation in the 1970s and '80s. Nairn's is now Forbo-Nairn Ltd and still performs its magic in Den Road.

KIRKCALDY BRUSH FACTORY.

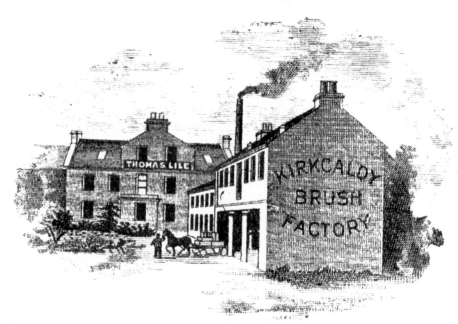
Opposite: The Raith Estate gave up much of its lands to housing, but Raith House, seen here in an early postcard, is still a home and has not succumbed to the fate of many of the other large houses in Kirkcaldy which have become hotels and nursing homes. *(JS)*

Kirkcaldy grew substantially during the nineteenth century, largely by incorporating Linktown, Pathhead, Sinclairtown and Gallatown, which made it 'The Lang Toun' for real. The first motor car was seen in Kirkcaldy in 1897 – one year after they were allowed on the roads. But motorised transport was a luxury and hardly for the common citizenry. Nor was the road system ready for it. Many of Kirkcaldy's streets still turned to mud in the rain and a programme began in 1900 to lay the main roads as 'causeways' with granite setts – Whytescauseway is a case in point. The Victoria Road Viaduct was finished in 1902 and the first installation of electric lighting came the same year – almost fifty lamps were erected between the top of The Path and the end of The Links. Factories, shops and other commercial premises flocked to sign up for the new source of light and power, and it led directly to the introduction of a tram service, which was inaugurated on the last day of February 1903. This linked central Kirkcaldy with Gallatown in one direction and Linktown and Invertiel in the other. Although the total population of Kirkcaldy was only around 35,000, the novelty of the trams was such that in their first three months they carried half a million passengers. In 1908 the tram system was extended as far as Leven. When this picture was taken Davidson's had a printing and wholesale stationery shop at 111 High Street. This address is currently a building society and opposite is the entrance to the Mercat. (DS)

St Brycedale's, shown here c. 1904, has since merged congregations with the Old Kirk (seen on the left of the picture, further down the hill). See also pages 80 and 81. (JS)

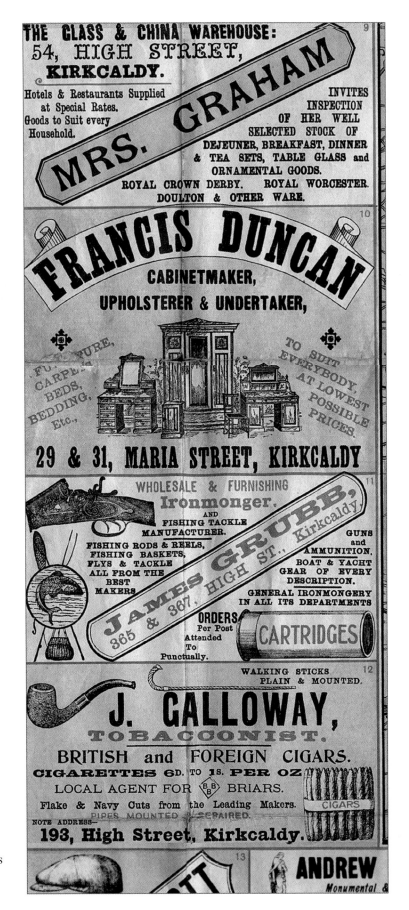

Many famous businesses are long gone, including Graham's china shop and Grubb the ironmongers. *(JS)*

There was a real feeling of civic confidence at the beginning of the twentieth century, exemplified by the new public buildings that sprung up in the town centre. The Adam Smith Halls (above) and Beveridge Halls had opened in 1899, both bequeathed by Provost Michael Beveridge, who had also given the lands for the Beveridge Park a few years earlier. The General Post Office (now a theme pub) was built on the corner of Wemyssfield and Hunter Street in 1900, and in 1902 the new police station opened next to St Brycedale Church. Two new churches were built – the gothic St Marie's (Our Lady of Perpetual Succour at the corner of Dunnikier Road and Victoria Road) and the landmark red St Andrews Church in Victoria Road. New schools were also built to service the growing population: the Elementary High School was added on to the existing High School (built in 1895 to replace the old Burgh School) opposite St Brycedale Church, plus Viewforth High School. Gallatown Primary and North Primary schools were also built. Balwearie golf course, Kirkcaldy's first, opened in 1906. The King's Theatre (later the Opera House, then the Regal, then the ABC) opened in 1904 and closed its doors as a cinema in 2001 in the face of increasing competition from multiplexes. This leaves Kirkcaldy without a cinema for the first time in over a century, except for the occasional movies shown in the Adam Smith Theatre as the building is now known. Note the absence of walls and gates in the later picture below. *(JS)*

Another mark of Kirkcaldy's growing confidence and prosperity at the end of the Victorian era was the opening of the Station Hotel, depicted in this 1903 advert. Built adjacent to the Adam Smith Halls by 'a private company of Gentlemen', it is now a private nursing home. *(JS)*

Linktown, or 'The Links', was once an independent settlement. Now it links Kirkcaldy town centre with Invertiel. The rather depressing discount centre stands on the site of old linen and pottery factories. This is where the Links Market would have been until the inauguration of the tram service necessitated its move to Sand Road (now the Esplanade). Opposite Stocks Discount Centre is an old building which has found a new use (below). The Raith Church enjoyed a brief respite as Raith Youth House and is now a children's play centre. *(DS)*

Aye, they knew how to enjoy themselves then! The author's mother showing her paces behind Marion Street, Linktown, on an unspecified date during the Late Conflict. *(BD)*

The old Philp Hall was one of a number of schools provided by local benefactor and linen manufacturer Robert Philp. He established a trust for the education of 400 children, which also bought books, clothes, shoes and tools for former pupils to start a trade. His money came initially from buying cloth from home weavers and selling it at markets, and later from his own weaving, spinning, bleaching and dyeing business at West Mills. A bachelor, he bequeathed his £75,000 fortune to the public good, largely out of annoyance at his heir and second cousin, missionary Dr John Philip, who had added an extra letter to his name – 'If my name isn't good enough for him, neither is my money,' Philp said. Robert Philp died in 1824 but his schools survived from 1828 until 1890. 'Philpers', as the ex-pupils became known, revered their benefactor. For many years they met on the anniversary of his death and walked in procession to his grave at the Old Kirk, where they each left a rose and received a penny bun. The building itself became a community hall and a school for what would now be called special needs. Demolished in 1965–6, it was replaced by a charmless concrete building. *(DS)*

High Street from opposite the Wemyss Building some time after 1900 (above) and in 2000 (below). West End Church (on the left) stands today, but the spire of the church on the right is gone and the frontage is covered by a modern edifice which recently housed a video store, now moved a few doors further west. The tram and horsecart have been supplanted by cars and controversial parking spaces, and most of the buildings in the foreground have been replaced. *(above, DS; below, BD)*

Local traders bedecked their buildings for Victoria Day – their affection for the queen was genuine and when she died in 1901 the town bell and church bells tolled for a full hour. Flags flew at half mast on public buildings, shops, factories and some houses, and the police wore black armbands. The provost had suggested that all shops and businesses close from 11 a.m. to 2 p.m. on the day of the funeral, but the shopkeepers and pub licensees decided to close for the whole day. However, individual licensed grocers opened for some time in the morning and did considerable trade, as did those pubs and licensed premises outside the burgh in Linktown, Gallatown, Pathhead and Sinclairtown, which opened their doors. *(DS)*

The High Street has seen its share of parades. The annual Cycle Parade later transmuted into the Pageant with the same tradition of dressing up and bedecking your bike. Here the revellers are travelling past Barnet & Morton's famous emporium in 1900. *(DS)*

Quite a rogues gallery, from a 1901 illustration of Kirkcaldy's great and good. *(JS)*

Clockwise from top left:
Michael Barker Nairn (later Sir Michael Nairn) was one of the most prominent local industrialists and public benefactors. Born in 1838, he inherited a thriving business. In 1821 the powerloom had arrived in Kirkcaldy – the first town to use it – and revolutionised the weaving industry but heralded doom for the hand weavers. His father, a ship sails weaver called Michael Nairn, built a factory in 1847 to manufacture floor-cloths, which were a great success and added to Kirkcaldy's prosperity. After 1876 Nairn's started to manufacture linoleum. The odour of the linseed oil used in the process hung over the town and gave it the distinctive 'Queer-like smell' celebrated in the famous poem (page 45). Nairn was chairman or a member of almost every important body in Kirkcaldy including the School Board, the YMCA and magistracy. He presented a school, the Cottage Hospital and other benefices to the town before he died in 1915.

A.R. Young of Methven's potteries (see page 54).

Michael Beveridge was an exact contemporary of Sir Michael Nairn but died of pneumonia in 1890 at the age of fifty-four. His fortune derived from the linoleum business of Shepherd & Beveridge. Married twice, he died childless but his legacy was evident at the beginning of the new century. Provost from 1886, Beveridge left £50,000 for a park, the Adam Smith Halls and a library. He also built substantial houses at the top of Bennochy.

John Barry was an employee of Shepherd & Beveridge (an offshoot of Nairn's) but he and Ostlere left in 1881 to set up their own business at Forth Avenue (page 45). Nine years after the death of Michael Beveridge, James Shepherd (see below) joined and the company became Barry, Ostlere & Shepherd. They bought many other businesses and buildings, and at one point had twelve factories in the town. The firm closed in 1964 and the site of the factory is now occupied by a nursing school, an hotel and a car dealer's premises.

John Lockhart owned the Links Linen Factory. His grandfather, Ninian Lockhart, who established the business, was reputed to rise before dawn and take his cloths on foot to markets in Perth and Dundee. The business continued at the same factory until 1981. Ninian's son (also called Ninian) set up a separate spinning business at Bennochy Works (now the site of Abbotsmill, page 81). He died in Whyte House in 1880 but the business continued into the 1980s.

Lewis Grant was a partner in Douglas & Grant, an engineering company. Its Dunnikier Foundry was best known for its 1863 Corliss Engine, the first ever produced in Britain, and a long line of mill and ship engines.

Peter Herd The firm of Water Herd & Son operated a number of mines, including the Begg at Clunie and the Dunnikier at Kirkcaldy.

James Henry Dalziel (Lord Dalziel of Kirkcaldy) held the

M. B. Nairn, Esq. J.P., of Rankeilor and Dysart

A. H. McIntosh, Esq. J.P., Victoria House

parliamentary seat of Kirkcaldy Burghs for the Liberals in four elections from 1892 to 1900, beating off the Unionist challenge – including Michael Nairn who stood against him in 1900. He remained in Westminster until his resignation in 1921. Politics had always been keen in Kirkcaldy, with the Melvilles of Raith taking the Whig (Liberal) interest against the Oswalds of Dunnikier who

Abbotsford
& Sons)

THE LATE PROVOST BEVERIDGE, J.P.,
Beechwood

John Barry, Esq., J.P., Bennochy Park

ains

of Industry

John Lockhart, Esq., J.P., Terracebank

J. H Dalziel, Esq., M.P. for Kirkcaldy Burghs

Rossend Castle

Peter Herd, Esq., Whytebank

Lewis Grant, Esq., J.P., Albert Road

were of the Tory (Conservative and Unionist) persuasion. Control of the Burgh passed between them in turn.

James Shepherd of Shepherd & Beveridge and later Barry, Ostlere & Shepherd (see opposite) lived at Rossend Castle in Burntisland from 1873 (page 19). He had originally been technical manager (and later a partner) at Nairn's.

Alexander H. McIntosh originally came to Kirkcaldy to work for Samuel Barnet & Son, a joinery business in the Links, in 1850 when he was nineteen. Fifteen years later he left to start his own business and by 1880 he had built a large factory in Victoria Road. McIntosh had been astute enough to include his own railway siding on the site and he prospered, soon taking over the adjacent Keys engineering works.

The Victoria Cabinet Works partly fitted out the *Queen Elizabeth* and *Queen Mary* and was deeply involved in war work. McIntosh furniture was a byword for quality and style. With the growing importance of road transport over rail, the company was able to move to Mitchelston in 1970 and a later merger sprouted the present-day firm ESA-Mcintosh.

Lino

Much of Kirkcaldy's fame and fortune rests on linoleum. Born from the floor-cloth, weaving and sail-making industries with their supply of skilled workers, the first lino works – Nairn's, 1876 – also created indirect employment for coalminers, printers, cork-cutters, engineering factories and other trades. Local shops and other business also benefited from the prosperity of the town and the workers. Michael Nairn, born in 1804, was the third son of James Nairn and came from a family of master weavers. Nairn initially opened a canvas-weaving business in Coal Wynd in 1828, supplying canvas to floor-cloth manufacturers in England and taking advantage of the adjacent harbour.

He decided to start his own floor-cloth company in 1847. Borrowing £4,000 to build his first factory was a major risk since floor-cloth took months to mature and dry in sunlight before it could be sold. The factory with its large south-facing windows in Nether Street on top of Pathhead was known as 'Nairn's Folly' and showed no profit for two years. Michael was a hard worker, travelling extensively to sell his cloth, and he died of exhaustion in 1858 aged fifty-four.

After his death his widow, son Robert and manager James Shepherd formed a partnership and in 1861 they were joined by the founder's other son, Michael Barker Nairn (page 42). The 'Folly' was extended, new technology introduced and at the 1862 Exhibition in London and the 1867 Paris Exhibition Nairn's won several prizes. By 1874 there were five floor-cloth manufacturers in Kirkcaldy in addition to Nairn's and by 1877 Kirkcaldy had become the world's largest producer of linoleum.

Shepherd & Beveridge was formed in 1864 as a partnership between James Shepherd (ex-Nairn's) and Michael Beveridge, who had worked in the insurance business in London and was later Provost of Kirkcaldy. Their Kirkcaldy Floor-cloth Works was badly damaged by fire in 1868 and had to be rebuilt. In 1873 Shepherd was rich enough to buy the old Durie home of Rossend Castle and to pay for the site of the Carnegie Library in Burntisland. His partner died in 1890 and in 1899 he joined Barry & Ostlere.

The other important manufacturers were Hendry, Whyte & Strachan's National Floor-cloth Works, founded in 1869; the North British Floor-cloth Co., established in 1872 at Sinclairtown; the Patent Floor-cloth Co., started in 1873 by John Whyte (another former manager at Nairn's) and Robert Douglas of the Kirkcaldy engineering company Douglas & Grant with backing from Ayrshire shipowners – a fire in 1880 sent the company into liquidation; Tait, Chorley & Co.'s Caledonian Floor-cloth Works, opened in 1874 by John Tait, a former butler for Oswald of Dunnikier – this company became Tait, Cairns & Co. in 1883; and Barry, Ostlere & Shepherd, formed in 1899.

In 1902 the daily output of lino, cork carpet, floor-cloths and other material from all Kirkcaldy factories exceeded 143,000 square yards – almost a quarter of a mile square or enough to provide a 2-foot-wide covering all the way to Glasgow and back. But it was Nairn's (now Forbo-Nairn, page 79) that became synonymous with linoleum and with Kirkcaldy.

THE QUEER-LIKE SMELL!

Boiling linseed oil to make linoleum cement produced the typical smell – and since most factories were near the railway lines through the town or around the station, the smell was most noticeable when approaching by train. This inspired the famous poem penned by Mary Campbell Smith.

The Boy in the Train

Whit wey does the engine say Toot – toot?
Is it feart to gang in the tunnel?
Whit wey is the furnace no pit oot
When the rain gangs doon the funnel?
What'll I hae for my tea the nicht?
A herrin', or maybe a haddie?
Has Gran'ma gotten electric licht?
Is the next stop Kirkcaddy?

There's a hoodie-craw on yon turnip-raw!
An' seagulls! – sax or seeven.
I'll no fa' oot o' the windae, Maw,
It's sneckit, as sure as I'm leevin'.
We're into the tunnel! We're a' in the dark!
But dinna be frichtit, Daddy,
We'll sune be comin' to Beveridge Park,
And the next stop's Kirkcaddy!

Is yon the mune I see in the sky?
It's awfy' wee an' curly.
See! there's a coo and a cauf ootbye,
An' a lassie pu'in' a hurly!
He's chakkit the tickets and gien them back,
Saw gie me my ain yin, Daddy.
Lift doon the bag frae the luggage rack,
For the next stop's Kirkcaddy!

There's a gey wheen boats at the harbour mou'.
An eh! dae ye see the cruisers?
The cinnamon drop I was sookin the noo
Has tummelt and' stuck tae ma troosers . . .
I'll sune be ringin' ma Gran'ma's bell,
She'll cry, 'Come ben, my laddie.'
For I ken mysel' by the queer-like smell
That the next stop's Kirkcaddy!

The linoleum factories clustered around the station used the railways to bring in coal and raw materials and to export finished goods. The large complex in this picture is Barry, Ostlere & Shepherd's works. The site is now occupied by Dundee University's College of Nursing and Midwifery. Rail freight largely stopped in the 1950s and was gone completely by 1984. *(JS)*

The main preoccupations in Kirkcaldy during the tumultuous decade between 1910 and 1919 were women worker's rights, better housing and – of course – the war. In 1911 women weavers went on strike in support of co-workers sacked for demanding a wage increase and union recognition rather than victimisation. The townspeople flocked to cheer them when fifteen of their number were fined for disorderly conduct, and the mood was such that this and further strikes led to better wage increases in local factories. Among the causes of the unrest were poor housing conditions. These agricultural workers' houses at Boglilly Cottages were typical. *(DS)*

Almost 2,000 new homes were built between 1900 and 1919, including those near Beveridge Park, around Pratt Street, in Sinclairtown and Gallatown, plus cottages in Dunnikier Road and Ava Street and villas in Townsend Place, Loughborough Road, Abbotshall Road and Beveridge Road. However, the poorer sections of the community still suffered appalling conditions and no rent control. Nicol Street, shown here, was a case in point with its three-storey houses, pipe-clay closes and shared toilets. Built in the 1870s as 'New Town' to accommodate overspill from Linktown as workers in the linen and pottery factories clamoured for housing, this street took its name from a local linen company. These houses in turn were taken down in the 1960s and 1970s to be replaced by more modern dwellings. Peggie's Pub later made way for the Novar Bar. *(DS)*

Much of the discontent with living conditions stemmed from the malaise created by the First World War. Kirkcaldy had been heavily involved with war work – iron foundries made munitions, linen factories made uniforms, McIntosh's furniture company built aeroplane wings at its Victoria Road premises, the Royal Navy used Ravenscraig Castle as an munitions store, the American Navy took over the harbour, more than 7,000 of Kirkcaldy's young men joined the forces and almost 1,000 died. New house building was stalled for the duration. The government appeased the population with a promise of 'homes fit for heroes' after the war, but little materialised. In 1919 local authorities were allowed to build their own houses for the first time, but the subsidies were so meagre that Kirkcaldy constructed fewer than 200. Terraced homes like these at Nether Street were replaced by high-rise flats in the 1960s and Mid Street has been largely replaced by new housing. *(DS)*

Parades were a great diversion. Barnum & Bailey's circus came to town in 1902. *(DS)*

Above: The harbour was improved at a cost of almost £150,000 between 1904 and 1908 with the addition of an outer harbour and a gated inner basin, but not entirely in line with Sir John Coode's 1884 plan. The arrangement remains today although the gate is no longer there. The building with the crow-stepped gable is Sailors Walk. One of Kirkcaldy's oldest buildings, erected in the sixteenth century by a merchant, it was restored in 1952. *(DS)*

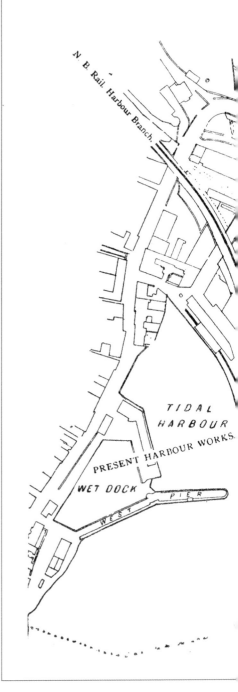

SIR JOHN COODE'

OF

PROPOSED HAR

N. B. Rail. Harbour Branch.

TIDAL HARBOUR

PRESENT HARBOUR WORKS.

WET DOCK

WEST PIER

Coode was the foremost authority on harbours of his day and he submitted a plan which was haggled over, discussed and finally voted on at a mass meeting at the Adam Smith Halls in 1903. *(JS)*

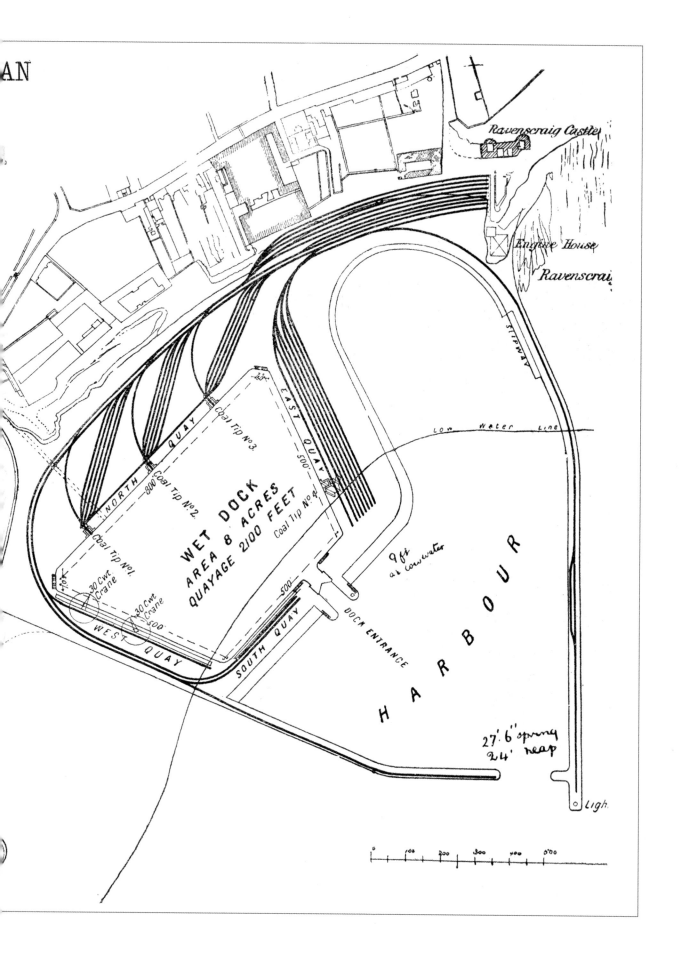

AN

Ravenscraig Castle

Engine House

Ravenscrai

SLIPWAY

LOW WATER LINE

Coal Tip No3.

Coal Tip No2.

EAST QUAY

500'

NORTH QUAY

300'

WET DOCK
AREA 8 ACRES
QUAYAGE 2100 FEET

Coal Tip No 4

Coal Tip No1.

9 ft
at lowwater

HARBOUR

30 Cwt
Crane

30 Cwt
Crane

500'

WEST QUAY

500'

DOCK ENTRANCE

SOUTH QUAY

27' 6" spring
24' neap

Ligh.

0   100   200   300   400   500

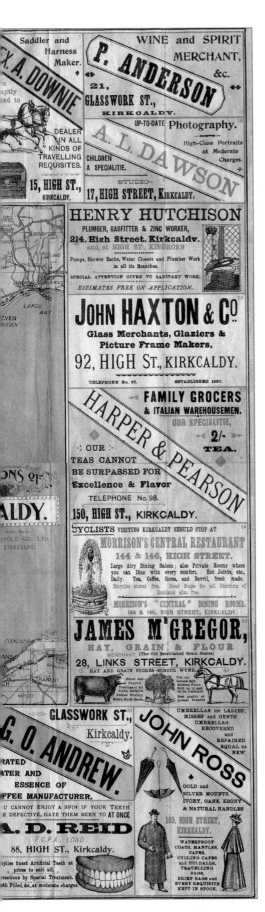

This local map was squarely aimed at the many cyclists who passed through or started out from Kirkcaldy. It was sold as a promotional vehicle (if that's the word) by Neilson's, the bicycle company, which later became Neilson's Garage, and includes cycling-related adverts (Morrison's Restaurant, for example) as well as others of a general nature. A lot of these businesses survived until late on in the twentieth century. Grubb's, for instance, only closed in 2000, albeit operating from different premises. Clark the coal merchant's logo could still be seen on Lila Cottage at Bennochy until recently although the business was long closed. *(JS)*

The Esplanade or Promenade ('The Prom') is Kirkcaldy's strand. In earlier times, children collected sea coal, mostly at the west end facing Linktown, the area known as The Bucket Pats (above) or further along near Port Brae. Coalmining was still taking place in Kirkcaldy in the 1920s, but the Pannie Pit, near Smeaton Road, ceased production in 1929 after almost fifty years. Seafield Colliery was proposed, but took years to come to fruition. Kirkcaldy returned its first Labour MP, Thomas Kennedy, in 1921 in the great post-war sweep of the Labour Government. This administration took housing more seriously than its predecessors and council house building started in earnest. Hayfield, Winifred Street, King Street and the Balfour Street area were examples of well-designed semi-detached homes in tree-lined, often curved streets. The greatest change to Kirkcaldy came with the construction of the sea wall and the creation of the Esplanade or Promenade beside it. The sea wall, though greatly needed to prevent the frequent floods, was mainly conceived as a solution for high unemployment. It was completed in 1922, but it was years before the government reimbursed Kirkcaldy for the costs – over £80,000 – as promised. The sea wall and Esplanade (opened in 1923) replaced Sand Road, which often flooded and was uniformly considered a disgrace to the town. *(DS)*

Opposite, above: This rather whimsical drawing of the Battery at Sand Road during a sea flood shows how necessary a sea wall was. Volunteer's Green, as it was known, was originally part of a 9-acre site granted by Charles I in 1644 for drying and bleaching linen, but was gradually eaten into by encroaching development until less than an acre remained. Drilling took place here from 1860 when Volunteer Companies were formed of soldiers returning from the Crimea. The volunteers moved to Kinghorn in 1901. *(JS)*

Opposite, below: The importance of the sea wall can also be seen in this March 1989 photograph where the south-east wind and the spring tides combine to swamp the Esplanade. The storms did considerable damage to the sea wall. The picture also shows the twin winding towers of Seafield Colliery months before their demolition and some 1980s building, including the multi-storey car park, known locally as Fort Apache, to the left of The Mercat shopping centre. *(DS)*

The 1920s and 1930s also saw the end of Kirkcaldy's pottery industry. It began in 1714 with the manufacture of brick and tile using clay from a pit near where Balwearie School now stands. Later, the focus shifted to domestic and ornamental wares, with four potteries working. Kirkcaldy was an ideal location for the pottery industry because of the excellent local clay and a ready supply of water, coal and salt (for glazing), and the harbours of Kirkcaldy and nearby Dysart for export. Later, a light railway took the clay from Balwearie across Pratt Street to the Links Pottery. The tunnel is used today as a passageway into the grounds of Balwearie School. David Methven & Son, which made mainly domestic pottery after its brick and tile works closed at the end of the nineteenth century, was one of four major Kirkcaldy potteries. Methven's pottery in Linktown was a huge complex by any standards. The factory in Methven Road (originally Pottery Road) had a showroom on the frontage of Links Street and the works behind. This picture shows some of the women workers, including the author's Auntie Nellie, front left. *(KYL)*

The famous Wemyss cats cost 7s 6d in the 1920s but now change hands at auction for over £10,000. *(KYL)*

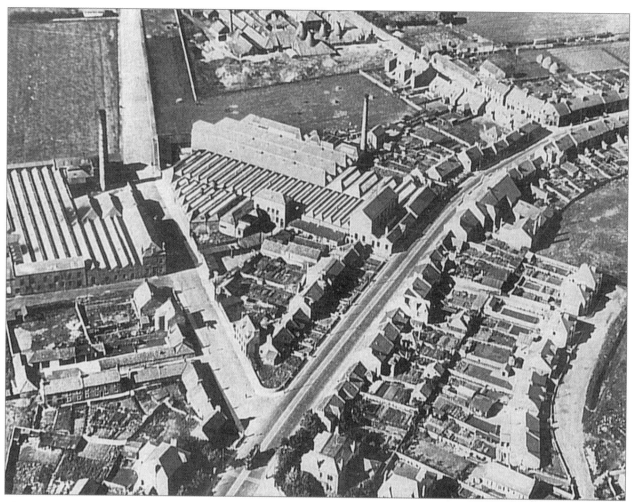

Three smaller potteries were founded in the Gallatown area during the nineteenth century, starting with Robert Methven Heron's Fife Pottery and later the Sinclairtown and Rosslyn Potteries. Heron's Fife Pottery, famous for its Wemyss Ware, was the best known. Wemyss Ware, the most attractive and sought-after Scottish earthenware pottery, was produced from around 1882 to 1930 and named after the Wemyss family who were early patrons. Its most distinctive characteristic is the free-flowing, naturalistic hand-painting and the choice of shapes. In addition to the famous Wemyss cats (opposite) there were pigs, tableware and everyday items decorated in bold colours with fruit, animals, birds and flowers, especially roses. The artist mainly responsible for the designs was Karel Nekola, a Bohemian who trained at Dresden and was recruited by Robert Methven Heron to work in Fife. Esther Weeks, the last Wemyss decorator, was taught by Karel's son Joseph. Each design was painted directly on to the biscuit-fired pottery. The glaze had to be fired at a relatively low temperature which allowed for more subtle effects. The labour required and the high discard rate in the kiln made Wemyss Ware expensive, but it was popular with the rich. When the Fife Pottery closed in 1930 the rights and moulds were bought by Bovey Pottery in Devon, which continued to produce it until the late 1950s. This aerial photograph shows the extent of the Fife Pottery site around the time of closure. Rosslyn Street runs across the picture, with the tram at the junction with Park Road. Virtually no trace of these potteries now exists.

George MacLaughlan's Sinclairtown Pottery started life in Rosslyn Street in 1869 and later moved to nearby Oswald Road. Rosslyn Pottery, also in Oswald Road, was opened in 1879 by two ex-Methven employees, potter William Crawford and travelling salesman Adam Morrison. All four stopped working between 1928 and 1932 because of the economic conditions created by the Depression and declining clay reserves. *(KYL)*

Lino magnate Michael Nairn's son, the second Sir Michael, succeeded him but by 1930 he and Lady Nairn had disposed of most of the estate, leaving only Dysart House and its gardens. The rest of the estate became the property of the town and Ravenscraig Park was donated to the Council on condition that it be used as a public park. Dysart House became a carmelite convent. *(BD)*

The most important event in Kirkcaldy in the early 1930s was the incorporation of Dysart, which up until the beginning of the decade had been a separate burgh. The first church in Dysart was dedicated to St Serf, who died in 543. In his time it belonged to a monastic order. It was rededicated on 26 March 1245 by Bishop David de Bernham, who was responsible for the rededication of many ancient Fife churches at this time, including Kirkcaldy's Old Kirk. The ecclesiastical parish embraced the Burgh of Dysart, Pathhead, Sinclairtown, Gallatown, Boreland, and part of Thornton. The name Dysart derives from *diseart*, meaning a religious retreat. *(BD)*

So important were Dysart and other Scottish ports for the North Sea trade that Campvere near Antwerp gave Scottish sailors the privilege to enter the town without paying the tolls which were imposed on other countries' crews. This is the origin of the term 'Scot-free'. Coalmining had been carried out in Dysart since at least the fourteenth century and coal was exported by sea from 1450. Now the traffic is mainly pleasure boats. St Serf's is under restoration in the lower picture. *(NGB, above; BD, below)*

Salt was also a major export commodity for Dysart. The availability of coal made the salt pan drying process economic, and there was great trade with Scandinavia and the Low Countries. Dysart was known as 'The Saut Burgh' for many years and the Scottish equivalent of 'carrying coals to Newcastle' was 'carrying saut tae Dysart'. Dysart's attractive Dutch-inspired houses with their red pantiles and crow-stepped gables are a reminder of those days – the ships, which could not sail back from Holland empty, were ballasted with roof tiles and later these were manufactured locally to the same pattern. The street names – Pan Ha', Hie Gait and Saut Girnal – are also reminders of the industrial past. The Dysart Trust was instrumental in the renovation of the houses pictured below in the 1960s and the Queen Mother visited them in 1969. *(CP)*

Dysart's most famous son is perhaps John MacDouall Stuart, who opened up Australia, leading six expeditions across the continent between 1858 and 1862 and finally travelling 2,000 miles from Adelaide to Darwin by way of Alice Springs and what is now Mount Stuart. MacDouall Stuart, born in Dysart in 1815, was orphaned at the age of ten when his customs officer father died. There was sufficient money for John to receive an education and later to train as a civil engineer in Edinburgh, and after working in Glasgow, he sailed for Australia in 1838. From 1844 to 1846 he was the surveyor with Captain Sturt's expeditions to define the geographical centre of the continent – for which he received the Royal Geographical Society medal in 1860 – but it was not until 1858 that he led the first of his own six treks into the Australian hinterland. The first three expeditions were purely land surveys. On the first, he travelled with six horses, two companions and an Aboriginal who deserted them. The 1862 expedition, some 2,000 miles from Adelaide to Darwin, was the most successful. The government of South Australia offered a prize of £2,000 to the first person to traverse the continent, which started a race. Two other explorers, Burke and Wills, reached the north the year before MacDouall Stuart, but had taken a shorter route and died on the return journey south. Stuart was accorded a hero's welcome on his return to Adelaide. With his prize, and with his health shattered by the expeditions, he returned to Glasgow in 1864, then moved to live with his widowed sister in London. He died two years later and is buried in Kensal Green Cemetery. A museum was installed in his Dysart house (below) by Kirkcaldy District Council with help from the National Trust in 1977. *(BD)*

Dysart Tolbooth was built in the 1570s. Cromwell's troops lodged there and one blew the roof off during a drunken spree by setting off gunpowder confiscated from a local merchant and stored in the tower. The adjoining Town Hall (1885) can be seen in this 1897 picture, taken around the time of Queen Victoria's diamond jubilee. *(DS)*

The wonderful art deco fire station opened in 1938, the same year as the ice rink in Gallatown. *(CP)*

The incorporation of Dysart in 1930 increased Kirkcaldy's population to almost 44,000 people and 11,000 homes. A further 1,300 houses had been built by the time war broke out in 1939. Boreland, further lands at Hayfield, Dunnikier Estate, Templehall, Mitchelston, Muirton, Pathhead Muir and Tyrie were all acquired for building by 1938 and some existing housing, such as in Linktown, was redeveloped. The last trams ran in 1931, the same year as the Girls' Club (YWCA) started on The Esplanade. Forth Park maternity hospital opened in 1935 and the next year the John Hunter Hospital was inaugurated, using the eminent physician's own house in Hunter Street and the money bequeathed and invested on his death in 1916 as a means to address the health problems of the poorer sections of the community. For over twenty years the building was the offices of the Inland Revenue. An abattoir was constructed in 1932 in what is now Oriel Road. By that time Kirkcaldy had no fewer than eight cinemas. The coronation of George VI in 1937 certainly gave everyone something to celebrate. *(DS)*

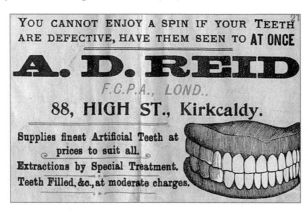

As ever in wartime, women found work in the factories alongside those men whose reserved status kept them out of the armed services. *(DS)*

The Second World War and Beyond

Kirkcaldy, like most towns, was completely taken up with the war and its aftermath. Women had always worked in the factories, but during wartime they were in the majority. A few men, those in 'reserved occupations', worked alongside them. They must have felt in a strong position – in October 1939 some 2,000 Nairn's workers went on strike to get union recognition, higher wages and better conditions. After 1945 there was an increased need for housing as the birth rate rose, servicemen returned and started families, immigrants, refugees and foreign soldiers stayed – especially Poles – and people lived longer. The years from 1946 to 1950 saw an explosion in house building – over 1,000 by the Burgh Council and some 350 by the newly established Scottish Special Housing Association (SSHA), mainly in Sauchenbush to house the influx of 100 miners and their families from the West of Scotland, promised jobs in the short-lived Rothes Colliery. The predictions of some older, experienced miners proved to be correct – Rothes turned out to have more water than coal.

There was no blitz as such on Kirkcaldy, despite the proximity of strategic targets like the Rosyth naval base and the Forth Bridge, and the importance of the town's factories in the war effort. The first bombing raid, a daylight attack on ships in the Forth in October 1939, went largely unheeded. Early one morning in July 1940 a dozen bombs were unaccountably dropped at Begg Farm, damaging the windows of the farm cottages blowing one man out of bed and killing two cows.

Air raid precautions were strongly in force. More than 1,600 townspeople joined the ARP and the Fire Wardens. The Local Defence Volunteers (LDV, later called the Home Guard or, more colloquially, Dad's Army) were almost 1,000 strong. A black-out prevented the enemy using Kirkcaldy's lights to guide them up the Forth, and concrete anti-landing defences were erected at strategic points along the coast. Gas masks were carried at all times, even by children. Food rationing was in force and continued into the 1950s, although flour and bread were not rationed until 1946 after a bad harvest and an appalling winter – for which many people blamed the new Labour government!

Many local firms stopped normal production to engage in war work. Just as it had in 1917, the furniture firm of McIntosh made wooden aeroplane parts at the Victoria Road works, and later diversified into coffins and ammunition boxes. Sir Michael Nairn, the linoleum manufacturer, turned his company's offices on The Path into a hospital. Nairn's had already applied its floor-covering know-how to the production of camouflage material, gas-proof tarpaulins, bitumenised coverings for bomb-damaged windows and doors, canvas for bunk beds to use in the London Underground air-raid shelters and 6 million pairs of gloves. By 1942 the factory was pressing fuel tanks for the famous Halifax bomber and later manufactured parts for Lancasters (page 64) and other aeroplanes, 25-pounder shells, torpedoes, gun mountings and bombs, including 6-ton Tallboys and 10-ton Grand Slams.

At least one local boy flew in bombers and dropped bombs partly made in Kirkcaldy. David Durie of Kinglassie (the author's father) is second left, shown here with his crew in Pathfinder Squadron. *(BD)*

The Town House, designed in 1937, was completed in 1956. During their visit in July 1958, the Queen and the Duke of Edinburgh attended a civic reception in the still-new building. This picture shows the Town Square, with the Sheriff Court (see page 4) in the background. *(FC)*

Opposite, above: The High School did its bit for the Second World War effort – including 'adopting' the crew of the *Belgique*, a Belgian merchant vessel, which berthed in Kirkcaldy harbour. The author's Aunt Edith is top left. Her hair's better these days. *(BD)*

Opposite, below: King George VI and Queen Elizabeth (now the Queen Mother) visited on 28 June 1948. *(FC)*

The original Burgh School in Hill Street (1725–1843) was the place of education of economist Adam Smith, architect Robert Adam and others, as a plaque shows. *(BD)*

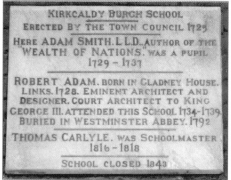

The site (above) is now a car park adjacent to the Fife Free Press offices. Thomas Carlyle was master there from 1816 to 1818 and by all accounts enjoyed his time before moving south to seek his fortune by writing histories and becoming 'The Sage of Chelsea'. He lodged across Kirk Wynd in a building (right) which was demolished in one of the many acts of civic vandalism that also swept away Adam Smith's house nearby in the High Street. *(BD)*

The site of Carlyle's lodgings later became the Trustee Savings Bank and more recently a pub. *(BD)*

Left to right: Thomas Carlyle in the company of his brother, his niece Mary Aitken and Provost Don Swan (1808–99), himself educated at the Academy and the Burgh School. Originally a flax-spinner, Swan first became Provost in 1841 and was at the centre of many improvements to Kirkcaldy's amenities. He was presented with his portrait in oils by a grateful citizenry in 1874. He remained a lifelong friend of Carlyle's. The picture was taken on the steps of Swan's then home, St Brycedale House in Hunter Street. *(JS)*

Adam Smith (1723–90), a Burgh School pupil, is regarded as the founding father of economics. He developed much of the theory of markets now seen as the basis for standard economic thought. His influence has been held to blame for much of the free-market excesses of the 1980s, but he was in fact more libertarian and social-minded than he is given credit for. He was born in Kirkcaldy where his father was Comptroller of Customs and had the unhappy experience when aged three of being stolen by gypsies. *(BD)*

By the 1840s it was obvious that the Burgh School was too small, so a new building was constructed further up the hill across St Brycedale Avenue in 1843 (above, *DS*). It was designed in line with the then popular classical or 'Greek' style. It taught to a good standard and was accorded 'Higher' status by virtue of its excellent examination results and good curriculum. By 1893 it had also become the 'High' school in name. Sir Michael Barker Nairn provided the funds – over £100,000 – and the well-known extravagant classical portico was retained but elevated by one floor (below left, *DS*). The new High School was notable for its modern conveniences, including a speaking tube by which the rector (headmaster) could communicate with the classrooms, and studs in the bannisters to prevent sliding! The Technical School was added in 1929. One of the most significant developments in the town in the post-war years was the building of the new Kirkcaldy High School at Dunnikier Level. Costing almost half a million pounds, it was a flagship for New Education and was visited by Queen Elizabeth and Prince Philip. The new High School's relatively remote location meant that buses had to be provided for pupils and many took school lunches – especially those from Kinghorn and Burntisland. When the High School moved to a new building and a new site on the edge of town in 1958, the old building became Kirkcaldy Technical College, addressing the further education needs of the town's growing and increasingly technology-based industries. Now Fife College of Further & Higher Education, it acquired its appalling Tower Block at the height of 1960s/'70s architectural folly – hardly a jewel on Kirkcaldy's skyline (below right, *BD*). It may be removed or reduced in height in the future.

In the early 1950s Kirkcaldy had a population approaching 50,000, but living in fewer than 15,000 houses, only half of which had bathrooms and 70 per cent indoor toilets. A new community at Templehall was built to house 9,000 people and by 1956 the eight-storey flats had been constructed in Valley Gardens. This growth required services – the shops at Dunearn Drive were built in 1956 and the new Templehall Junior Secondary School – erected as a temporary building – had to be enlarged by 1953 and given a permanent, brick-built extension in 1957. The primary schools were also feeling the strain – Valley Primary, built in 1953 to take 650 pupils, had more than 800 on its roll, so a new school, Fair Isle Primary, was built and Dunearn Primary was planned. Templehall Church had over 1,000 children on the Sunday School roll in 1958, said to be the largest in the country. Other schools in the town were also coping with the baby boom. In 1959 the West School in Milton Road had an unprecedented thirty pupils in Primary 1. A casual glance along the eager faces in this 1960s photograph reveals a Blues musician, a used-car salesman, a pilot, two merchant seaman, a geographer, two teachers and an author. Not a bad crop. *(BD)*

The hallmark of the 1920s in Kirkcaldy was revival. Both civic building and council housing boomed and there was a new spirit of commercial confidence. A technical school was built alongside the existing High School (it eventually became Kirkcaldy Technical College, then Fife College, page 70). The War Memorial Gardens plus the building which is now the Kirkcaldy Museum, Art Gallery, Library and War Memorial complex were built as a result of a gift from Sir John Nairn in memory of his son who fell in the Great War. He also gave the lands for Ravenscraig Park in 1929. The High Street, pictured here at Whytescauseway, bustled with traffic. The buildings are festooned with wiring for electric lights, trams and the new-fangled automatic telephones, introduced in 1925. The building on the corner eventually gave way, in 1937, to Burton's and the Plaza Ballroom above. For a time it was also the headquarters of the Cooperative Insurance Society.

By the mid-1950s, Kirkcaldy could boast five cinemas, almost 750 shops, a greyhound stadium, the beginnings of a new hospital (the Victoria Hospital on the site of the Infectious Diseases Hospital in Hayfield Road) and a new colliery – the sinking of Seafield began in May 1954. Like many other pipe-dreams of this era, Seafield never fulfilled its potential. It was supposed to provide work for 2,500 men for 150 years. Likewise, the plans for a 'Golden Mile' along the Esplanade evaporated and gave way to concrete and car parks and the plan for a sports stadium with 75,000 capacity, a full-size soccer and rugby pitch and an athletics track never materialised. However, the town did get a new bus station for town buses near the new Town House in 1959. The pre-war original Esplanade Stand, retained for country bus services, received a facelift with new bus bays and more shelters. Dysart got new housing and many of its older buildings were renovated. Linktown, partially redeveloped in the 1930s, was largely flattened and rebuilt.

Over half the workforce of 30,000 was engaged in linoleum manufacture, coalmining, textiles, construction work and distributive trades, and they thought the good times were here to stay. Little did they know the '60s were just around the corner. (DS)

The junction of Whytehouse Avenue and the High Street, with the famous Grahams China Shop in the foreground. This was the typical trysting place for young people who always arranged to 'meet at Grahams before the dancing'. The trams were long gone but the cobblestones were only lifted later. Further along at the bottom of Whytescauseway is the Burton's building – contrast this with the picture opposite.

The '60s was a period of controversy and contention in Kirkcaldy. A major retail redevelopment of the town centre was agreed in 1964 in the face of strong opposition. Most shopkeepers felt the existing provision was more than adequate: Marks & Spencer was in the High Street and British Home Stores opened its first shop in Scotland in Kirkcaldy. None the less, a round of compulsory purchases began on properties between the High Street and the Esplanade. The inevitable public inquiry delayed approval for the shopping centre scheme until 1967 and further delays held off the building of The Mercat until 1971.

By 1961 the town's population stood at over 52,000 and continued to grow. New housing – including the Ravenscraig flats and the idiosyncratic five-storey 'maisonettes' at Glamis Road, Bridgeton and elsewhere – added to the housing stock of 17,500 and improved its quality. No wonder, then, there was a crying need for a new extension to Forth Park Maternity Hospital, completed in 1966.

In 1963 the High Street saw parking restrictions for the first time, and two years later it became one-way between Whytescauseway and Port Brae. As if to underline the growing importance of car travel the completion of the Forth Road Bridge in 1964 was quickly followed by the opening of the Tay Road Bridge in 1967 and Sinclairtown train station closed in 1968, although there are now moves to reopen it.

In 1965 Barry, Ostlere & Shepherd, a major linoleum manufacturer, closed with 1,500 jobs lost. However, Seafield Colliery finally started production after more than ten years preparatory work and began setting new records. The Victoria Hospital, twelve years in the making, was finally completed in 1967. It replaced the old hospital near Ravenscraig Castle which had been in use since 1890 and was demolished to make way for The Kyles housing development in the 1980s. The swimming pool opened in 1969 and the days of sea bathing in the Lido or the harbour outer basin were over. And if there were only three cinemas – the ABC and the Odeon in the High Street and the Rio in St Clair Street – there were ample opportunities for dancing at the Raith and the Burma. (DS)

The Prom is best known as the site of the annual Links Market, first granted a charter as a weekly market in 1304. It is now a street fair, albeit reputedly the largest and longest-running of its kind in Europe. This picture also shows the construction of the Eight Storey Flats in the 1960s, with the Links Market stretching from Alexander's bus garage to Charlotte Street and the Country Bus Station in the distance. *(DS)*

Richard Cutland at the Links Market in gentler times, *c.* 1950. *(BD)*

The 1970s was the decade Kirkcaldy town centre radically changed. The Mercat and its associated multi-storey car park, both the subject of much planning controversy in the 1960s, started construction in 1971. Safeway opened on the site of Neilson's Garage at the other end of the High Street in 1975. Then in 1978 Phase II of The Mercat began. Work also started on The Postings and a new store for William Low (now Tesco) between Hunter Street and Hill Street, adjacent to the bus station. Both developments were to wait until the '80s for completion and when Mercat Phase II was opened in 1983 it stood almost unoccupied for more than a year. Kirkcaldy District Council came into being in 1975 with local government reorganisation which abolished the Burgh Council and headquartered Fife Regional Council in Glenrothes. The old Baillie's lamps which had stood outside the houses of senior councillors were collected together outside the Town House. *(BD)*

Overleaf: The miners' strike was the defining event of the 1980s, especially for a mining-dependent community like Kirkcaldy. When the Seafield Colliery towers were demolished in September 1989 it was a visible symbol of the death-knell which sounded for the mining industry across Scotland and the rest of the UK in the wake of the strike. The National Coal Board had announced in 1983 that Seafield would break even that year and even turn a profit for the first time. But in 1984 the National Union of Miners was cornered into a strike in the face of strong government determination to bring the union to its knees. During the dispute, Kirkcaldy miners at Seafield and Frances (with the exception of safety workers) had been almost unanimous in staying away. Near the end of the strike, the renamed British Coal indicated the impending closure of the Frances and the main face at Seafield, claiming that underground heatings were out of control. Eight hundred jobs went but Seafield struggled on. Despite increasingly bad relations between management and miners, in June 1987 it was said that Seafield was again heading for profitability and beating Scottish and UK coal production averages. But only six months later management reported massive losses and announced Seafield's closure. Open for just under thirty-five years, Seafield was supposed to have employed 2,500 men for 150 years. At the end there were only 650 miners. The two winding towers, famous Kirkcaldy landmarks and visible from miles away across the Forth, were brought down. The Frances pit was put into cold storage and it closed forever in the mid-1990s. Unemployment in Kirkcaldy – long above the national average – rose even higher. Now private housing stands where the Seafield winding towers loomed. More and denser housing is planned in the face of strong opposition. *(DS)*

Proposals first made in 1975 to pedestrianise the High Street from Whytehouse Avenue to the Port Brae were not popular with the Chamber of Commerce and High Street businesses. But temporary closures to traffic for four days became a regular feature of the Christmas period and full pedestrianisation happened in 1988 (sneaked in as an eighteen-month 'experiment'), but only as far as Kirk Wynd. As a result of the changed traffic patterns, the Port Brae received a major facelift in 1988, with a new layout where the High Street meets the Esplanade. The buildings east of the Port Brae pub on the corner of Coal Wynd were demolished to make way for a car park. *(DS)*

Up until the advent of motorised transport, horses pulled their loads up the long, steep trek of The Path to Nairn's and other factories. Coal was carried across the the Path Bridge which was removed, along with the Tollbooth, in the 1980s. The factory beyond the bridge is now a campus of Fife College of Further & Higher Education, the long weaving looms replaced by high-tech computer facilities. *(DS)*

Nairn's factories along Victoria Road and at Pathhead were demolished in 1981, clearing space used partly for new housing and partly still empty. Forbo-Nairn remains a major employer in the town. *(JS)*

Some of the history of the Old Kirk in Kirk Wynd has been told on page 30. In 1987 after fire damage to the church was repaired, the Revd John G. Sim led a re-dedication service. He then retired after forty-two years in the ministry but returned in September 1988 to carry out the dedication service for the new stained-glass windows which replaced those damaged in the fire. The windows, by Scottish stained-glass artist John Clark, commemorate the Old Kirk's restoration, and make a fine contrast to the Burne-Jones classics. The Old Kirk organ has an interesting history of its own and its share of troubles. Built and installed by August Gern of London – a Frenchman who crossed the Channel to build one organ and stayed on to build more, including ten in Scotland – it was inaugurated on Friday 2 October 1885 by Joseph Bradley, organist with the Hallé orchestra in Manchester. The organ used a new tubular pneumatic system driven by a patent hydraulic engine. The pulpit had to be moved forward to accommodate the organ which is behind it and between the stunning Burne-Jones memorial windows. In 1904 the centre tier of organ pipes was judged to be dangerous and during church improvements (including the installation of electric lighting) these pipes were replaced. In 1963 when church renovations were again being considered, a water tank burst and flooded the organ chamber. It was rebuilt by Jardine of Manchester at a cost of £3,000. During renovations to the church in 1968 the organ console was moved to its present location. However, a fire started by vandals in 1986 melted some of the organ pipes: the organ cost over £16,000 to repair and was valued at £175,000. The instrument is considered by musicians to be one of the best in the Fife. *(CP)*

Work on the spire of St Brycedale's. St Bryce is remembered in the area at the top of Kirk Wynd – St Brycedale – and the newer church there. In 1843 during the Disruption of the Church of Scotland, many clergy and laity left the national church in protest at the patronage system whereby local landowners chose the minister. They established a Free Church in Tolbooth Street, but soon outgrew it. A new church was planned at the top of Kirk Wynd, yards from the Old Kirk in 'open parkland on the outskirts of the town' donated by Provost Don Swan in 1876. It was designed to accommodate 1,150 people and included a ladies' room, a young men's hall to hold 150 (site of the famous Beacon Saturday Disco in the 1960s) and a Sunday School room for 300. The spire is 200 feet high and the architecture imitates thirteenth-century Gothic. Local stone was used – Fordell stone for the fabric and a hard stone from Gallatown Quarry for the inside walls of the tower. The church was officially opened in March 1881. In 2001 the congregations of the Old Kirk and St Brycedale merged. *(DS)*

Bennochy Mill, an old linen works dating from 1864, can be seen beside Abbotshall Church on page 4. It closed in 1982 and was demolished in 1985 to be replaced by a new complex of flats, Abbotsmill, which opened in 1987. *(BD)*

St Clair Street, the
beginning of
Sinclairtown (a reference
to the St Clairs of
Ravenscraig who owned
the land, see opposite)
was redeveloped in
1993. *(DS)*

At the same time
Commercial Street
received a facelift.*(DS)*

Ravenscraig Castle lies midway between the original royal burghs of Kirkcaldy and Dysart, now amalgamated. Building started in March 1460 on the orders of King James II (of Scotland) and it was constructed as an artillery fort to defend the Forth. It was used by his queen, Mary of Guilders, until her death. The castle was the first in the British Isles to be designed both to withstand bombardment and to have a platform for a counter battery. At Ravenscraig this platform faces out towards the River Forth which at the time of construction was infested with pirates and the destination for occasional forays by the English.

There was no such thing then as an architect – the master of work, David Boys, was a cleric who could read and write and who controlled the business, payments, materials purchase and the accounts on behalf of the owner. Under his direction the master mason (a man named Henry Merlzioun, pronounced Merlin) was responsible for the design and actual building, in conjunction with the master carpenter, Friar Andrew Lesouris, a lay brother of Cupar Abbey.

In the fifteenth century the red sandstone promontory stood much higher than now – the centuries have raised the beach around it. The promontory's face was also scarped at the time of building to form a perpendicular, inaccessible front. There is a cave at the foot of the scarp which was once large enough to accommodate a jetty and a barge for the use of the occupants of the castle, who could access it from inside. This barge is referred to in Sir Walter Scott's poem 'The Lay of the Last Minstrel'.

In 1470 King James III granted the castle and some tracts of local land plus a pension of 400 merks to William Lord Sinclair, Earl of Orkney, in exchange for the castle of Kirkwall and all his rights to the Orkney Islands. The Orkneys had been handed over to the Scottish crown as part payment of a dowry paid to James III's wife, daughter of King Christian of Denmark. Lord Sinclair came out of the deal badly, not only losing his rights on the Orkneys but also vast tracts of the northern counties of Caithness and Sutherland, which were potentially richer than Ravenscraig and its policies. His grandson became Lord Sinclair in 1489.

From this time until 1896 the castle remained in the possession of the Sinclairs, although it continued to be the destination for various royal excursions, notably as headquarters for King James V who sailed from Kirkcaldy to claim his French bride in 1536. During the English Civil War Parliamentarian troops under the command of Oliver Cromwell occupied the castle which had been used as a grain store by the local people, indicating that no one lived in it at that time (1651). In 1674 a party of Covenanters (Presbyterian dissenters) holding an illegal meeting at the castle were discovered by troops and arrested; some were banished to the plantations (i.e. the Carolinas). A report of 1794 said that the castle had been in a 'ruinous state and uninhabited for many years'. During the First World War its basement was used as an ammunition store and today it is under the care of Historic Scotland, which maintains the grounds and structure. The photograph shows its derelict state, and to the right, the high-rises and The Kyles, a modern housing development on the site of the old hospital. To the left is Path House, now a GP's practice and winner of conservation awards, and beyond are Nether Street and factories before redevelopment or demolition. (DS)

Marks & Spencer stands where the Town Hall once was, the tram lines are long gone, the main portion of the High Street from Whytescauseway to Kirk Wynd is pedestrianised and most of the old shop frontages have disappeared. The top picture faces south and west towards Whytescauseway and the lower towards the East End and the harbour. The concentration of spending in this area is such that there are now moves to revitalise – and possibly pedestrianise – the other end of the High Street and the area leading to the Port Brae. But who is shopping in all these new stores? Kirkcaldy's population in 1991 stood at fewer that 47,000 souls – lower than at any time since the 1940s and far below the 1961 peak of more than 52,000. *(DS)*

Balwearie Secondary School was built in 1964 on lands near the ruin of Balwearie Castle. This may or may not have been the home of Sir Michael Scott, 'the Balwearie Wizard'. Some say he was born as early as 1152 and others 1214. His death is recorded as 1234 in some documents and 1291 or 1300 in others. Sir Walter Scott, in 'The Lay of the Last Minstrel', places him far too late. We do know that he was actually one of the most learned men of his time. He was for a time the official Astrologer and Court Physician to that brilliant imperial heretic, Frederick II, and possessed a great knowledge of mathematics, alchemy and medicine. He is recorded as studying at Oxford, Paris and Toledo, where he learned enough Arabic to translate Aristotle's works. Scott's notoriety in the black arts was such that Dante placed him in the eighth circle of Hell in his *Inferno* among the magicians and soothsayers. It is also said that the Italian mathematician Fibonnaci studied under him and his contemporary Roger Bacon records his academic investigations in what we now call physics.

Scott's supposed wizardly exploits have intrigued storytellers since the thirteenth century. He is said to have set demons to cleave the Eildon Hills into three and to have set the Devil himself the impossible task of making a rope from the sand at Kirkcaldy harbour. His fury explains the frequent storms that lash the sea wall. Another story has Scott dispatched by Alexander III to ask the King of France to stop French pirates harassing the Scottish coast. Scott travelled to Paris in one night by going to the Bell Crag where the wizard had a cave created by the fires of hell. He summoned a horse no other man could ride and its fiery hooves left their impression in the sandstone as it leapt into the air and carried its master into the night sky. By sunrise the next morning horse and master were in Paris. The King took exception to the petition but Scott said: 'My horse will stamp its hoof three times. On the first stamp all the bells in Paris will ring. On the second stamp it will bring down the towers of this palace. If it stamps three times all Paris will fall.' The first two stampings had the predicted effect; before the third the King gave in and forbade French seaman from piracy against Scottish vessels. Michael returned to Scotland before the next day. Thereafter, the wizard would entertain his guests by magicking the choicest dishes straight from the kitchens of the King of France.

Scott also prophesied his own death from a falling stone and wore a metal helmet ever after. But he took it off in church and a stone fell from the ceiling, striking him on the head. Tradition varies concerning the place of his burial – some say Home Coltrame in Cumberland; others Melrose Abbey, where there is a effigy of him (above, *JS*). It is said that his books of magic are buried with him and many have tried to find them, usually to be frightened off by an apparition of some kind.

Overleaf: The twentieth century opened with almost £150,000 spent on improvements to the harbour, and finished with a derelict site and grandiose plans for exciting leisure, commercial, accommodation and marina developments. As one local wag had it: 'They'll be quaking in their boots in Monte Carlo when they see the plans for this lot.' The ships that came here as late as the 1980s are no longer able to berth. *(NGB)*

So where has Kirkcaldy come in the century or so since the Beveridge Park opened its gates? A population of around 35,000 has risen to over 50,000 and fallen back again by 3,000. However, the housing stock has doubled and all but a handful of homes have a bath or shower and an inside toilet. Half of the 20,000 households have a car and almost 3,000 of those two or more. Edinburgh and Dundee are less than an hour away by road or rail transport. But by contrast, all the cinemas are gone or going. The Raith, Plaza, Burma and other dance halls have become nightclubs or disappeared completely. No longer do bus drivers while away the time between runs in the Troc café. But once again people can walk in the High Street without being mown down by trams, cars or buses. The central section of the High Street has been remodelled, and hope springs eternal that the west and east ends will receive similar treatment and once again become places of thriving commerce – despite the car parking charges. Some green space – the grounds of Templehall School, the Cricket Pitch at Bennochy and the lands around the Priory – was lost to the increasing demand for housing. Jimmy Nicholl's football team shucked off its local nickname 'Raith Rovers Nil' and briefly played in the Premiership, took the Scottish League Cup and competed in Europe. But the harbour finally had to give up the ghost. For centuries it had nurtured and defined Kirkcaldy; now it is derelict. Great plans were announced for a marina, leisure complexes, waterfront restaurants and 'executive' housing. Little has come of this to date, with only a handful of planned apartments built. On the other hand, the retail park at Chapel, which accommodates Sainbury's, Halfords, Comet and other major chains, was a manifest success, even if it irritated the town centre traders and the occupants of the Mitchelston site a few miles along Chapel Level. A substantial housing development is planned nearby. And once again coalmining is on the agenda – albeit the unpopular and environmentally dubious surface and opencast variety. But most fundamentally, during the 1990s Kirkcaldy stopped being the centre of local government. The creation of Fife Council abolished royal burgh status and the centre of operations moved to Glenrothes. Through all of this Provost Beveridge's memorial has remained in Beveridge Park. *(DS)*

3
*Wemyss &
the Coaltowns*

The Michael pit near East Wemyss and the Bell pit at Coaltown of Wemyss were major mining
operations. In the 1860s the parish of Wemyss (which then included Buckhaven and Methil)
was producing between 50,000 and 60,000 tons of coal annually. The Wemyss Coal Company,
owned largely by the Wemyss family, was sufficiently wealthy to build its own railway between
the pits and the washery at Methil docks because its directors were not happy with the service
from the North British Railway. *(BD)*

This picture shows the considerable planning that went into 'Coaltowns', with adequate gardens and well-built houses. *(KYL)*

Opposite: The 'Haven Town of Wemyss', now West Wemyss, was created a burgh of barony in 1511. It was initially a port with salt pans and later a mining settlement. In 1985 the village was designated a conservation area because of its picturesque buildings including the eighteenth-century tolbooth, Wemyss Castle (*c.* 1420) and the salters' and colliers' houses. *(KYL)*

Overleaf: This aerial photograph shows the planned development of workers' homes in straight rows which contrast with the older, less rigid layout. *(KYL)*

The name of the Parish of Wemyss comes from the Gaelic 'Uiam' meaning a cave, which became 'Weim', then 'Weem' and finally the present 'Wemyss'. It is also found in the name Pittenweem (pages 119–20). Around 6000BC the sea formed a series of caves in the sandstone cliffs at Wemyss. In the following millennia the land rose and between 4000 and 3000BC the sea hollowed out another set of caves. They were occupied from the earliest times because of the shelter they provided and their proximity to the shore. The Wemyss caves contain carvings which indicate how long they have been occupied. The earliest symbols are the so-called cup markings in the Court Cave which date from the Neolithic or Bronze Ages (*c.* 3500–1000BC); their meanings are unknown. The main markings are Pictish (*c.* AD400–900) and are similar to the symbols found on Pictish stone slabs throughout the north and east of Scotland. Some symbols are representational – animals, birds, people, etc. – some are diagrammatic representations of objects such as combs, mirrors, cauldrons and swords, while others, such as 'tridents' and 'ships', may be merchants' marks. The caves also provided shelter for early Christian missionaries, as evidenced by fish carvings. The Vikings also left markings, including one in the Court Cave of Thor with his sacred hammer Mjolnir and his goat. The caverns containing carved artwork include the Court Cave, Dovecot Cave, Jonathan's Cave (or Factor's Cave) and the Sliding or Sloping Cave. They were first described by Professor James Young Simpson in 1865 and were first pictured in John Stuart's *Sculptured Stones of Scotland* in 1867. The Glass Cave, situated to the west of East Wemyss, was the site of one of the oldest glassworks in Scotland, established in 1610 by Sir George Hay (later Lord Kinnoul). It ran at a loss as the demand for glass was not high – the annual income was less than the monthly expenses. However, the works remained active and in 1698, David, 3rd Earl of Wemyss, obtained a patent from parliament giving him a monopoly on the manufacture of certain types of glass. In 1730 the owner went bankrupt and the works fell into ruin. *(KYL)*

The Coaltown murder. On 19 February 1909 young Michael Swinton Brown was followed into a lavatory in East Wemyss by Alexander Edminstone. He was murdered and robbed of £85 in money plus his watch and chain, but the story behind the crime is more fascinating that the bald facts. Brown was a clerk at East Wemyss and went to the bank every Friday to draw his company's wages. Edminstone, a 23-year-old unemployed miner, knew Brown's routine and followed him from the bank on to a tram. Why they went into the public lavatory together is not known, but Brown ended up strangled. The leather cash bag and the bank passbook were found on the shore near Macduff Castle. Edminstone had disappeared, so suspicion fell on him and he was traced to Strathmiglo, Perth and Glasgow. After a manhunt lasting several weeks throughout the whole of Britain he was found staying in a lodging house in Manchester under the name of Albert Edwards. A Gladstone bag in his possession contained £25 in single pound notes, 10 guineas in gold and £7 5s in silver. The man admitted to being Edminstone, but claimed that when he committed the crime he had not known what he was doing. At his trial on 8 and 9 July in Perth Circuit Court before Lord Guthrie, a defence of insanity was put forward. Certainly Edminstone had suffered from epileptic fits and his Advocate, Mr Christie, appealed to the jury to find him guilty of culpable homicide on account of diminished responsibility. After only ten minutes the jury returned a unanimous verdict of guilty of murder. Lord Guthrie passed sentence of death to be carried out at Perth Prison on 6 July. A petition to the Home Secretary asked that the sentence be commuted, but this was refused and Edminstone went to his fate. The considerable public and press interest the case generated is obvious from this photograph of sightseers at the scene of the crime. (KYL)

Coaltown of Wemyss was originally divided into Easter and Wester settlements but the villages grew together during the 1860s when the Wemyss Coal Company created a model village for workers at the nearby Bell pit. The attractive semi-detached miners' cottages are now part of a conservation area designated in 1980. *(KYL)*

The opening of the Co-op in 1930 was as big an event for Coaltown of Balgonie as the later closure of the pits. *(KYL)*

The opening of the Queen Victoria Memorial Hall, Coaltown of Balgonie in 1905. It was built by C.B. Balfour MP, a relative of Arthur Balfour, Prime Minister at the time, and owner of Balgonie mine. *(KYL)*

Coaltown of Balgonie is a late eighteenth-century mining and weaving village. It used the water provided by the Ore and Leven rivers which bound it. *(KYL)*

Like many mining villages, Coaltown of Balgonie boasted a brass band, along with pipe bands, pigeon clubs and other associations. *(KYL)*

4

Levenmouth

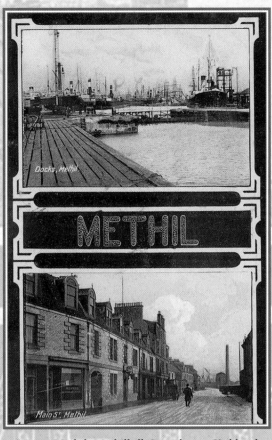

Leven, Methil, Methilhill, Innerleven, Kirkland,
Aberhill, Denbeath, Muiredge and Buckhaven
make up a large, urban, industrial area. *(BD)*

Buckhaven harbour, *c.* 1900. Buckhaven started out as a settlement of Norsemen in the ninth century and became primarily a weaving village and a fishing port. In the 1830s it was said to have the second-largest fishing fleet in Scotland with almost 200 boats. The fishing declined and after 1860 coalmining predominated. It also became a coastal holiday resort, despite the coal spoil which blackened the beaches. The same waste eventually silted up the harbour. In 1869 the locals bought an Episcopal Church from St Andrews and carried it stone by stone to Buckhaven. The building was restored in the 1980s as a theatre. *(DS)*

Buckhaven fire engine, *c.* 1900. *(DS)*

These photographs and the one opposite are taken from the official handbook of the 1909 Education Institute of Scotland Congress held in Kirkcaldy. They show Buckhaven Higher Grade School and give a quaint picture of what was considered a model education. By 1909 the population of the Parish of Wemyss – which included Buckhaven, Methil and Innerleven – had reached 25,000, including 5,000 children of school age. This, combined with the demand for a better technical education to serve the needs of local industry, necessitated a new school. As well as new elementary schools at East Wemyss and Denbeath, it was decided to upgrade Buckhaven Higher Grade School. The old school was demolished in a week and the new one erected in a matter of months. The 1,200 pupils got the benefits of new science labs, workshops, a hall for 'drill and gymnastics' and a 'room for cookery and laundry which is a model of what is needed for this course of instruction', according to Robert Suttie, then Chairman of the Wemyss School Board. *(JS)*

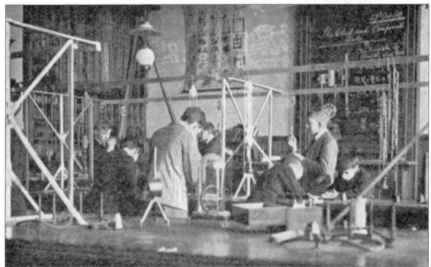

Methil's development was based on the docks which were built in the 1870s primarily to export coal from all over Fife. They were considered so remarkable that they were often the subject of postcards, such as these two from 1909. In addition to its three docks, Methil has a power station, a large leisure centre and a strong industrial base. Methil is a town with a strong sense of place and history – the Lower Methil Heritage Centre, opened in 1995, recalls the local industrial history. *(BD)*

A church was given to the Celtic Culdees of Loch Leven in the eleventh century and by the 1500s a harbour and a village had developed. Leven became a burgh of barony. The presence of the harbour stimulated many industries over the next 300 years – fishing, mining, weaving, spinning, textile bleaching, salt-panning and ropemaking. Shipping declined in the nineteenth century as the harbour silted up and the Methil Dock was built to the south. But the railway arrived and Leven – together with nearby Lundin Links and Largo – became a holiday, retirement and golfing centre in twentieth century. This postcard of Cock-My-Lane in 1904 is evidence of tourism. *(BD)*

Leven's long sandy beach became a popular destination in Edwardian times. Leased from the Durie Estate, the Esplanade, shown here in 1928, had a new concert hall and the road built two decades earlier brought trippers in their masses. Donkey rides, putting, sea-bathing and Pierrot shows were popular. The now-pedestrianised High Street, the swimming pool and leisure centre complex, the caravan site and the nearby parks such as Silverburn, with its woodland walks, gardens and a children's farm. *(BD)*

Upper Largo is an ancient village in the shadow of an extinct volcano called Largo Law. It grew around a twelfth-century church given to the Cistercian nuns of North Berwick by Earl Duncan of Fife. The church, shown above in a postcard from before the First World War, was consecrated in 1243 and refurbished in the seventeenth century when the spire was added. Inside is a model of the *Yellow Caravel*, the flagship of Sir Andrew Wood who defeated Henry VIII's fleet in 1498 off the coast. The churchyard has a Pictish symbol stone and the headstone of the family of Alexander Selkirk (see page 112). A popular holiday resort, Upper Largo attracted and continues to attract many visitors. Nearby beaches, golf and Keil's Den (below) were the main draws. Local legend always held that Largo Law was the site of buried treasure and in 1819 a tinker digging near Norries Law found a collection of silver Celtic ornaments. They were melted down for the metal but years later more items were found and are now on display in the Royal Scottish Museum, Edinburgh. *(BD)*

Adjoining Upper Largo, at the foot of a cliff on Largo Bay, is Lower Largo or Seatown of Largo. It was noted for fishing and the making of nets and knitted goods. Temple Hill, east of the village, is named for the land owned by the Knights Templar who were brought to Scotland in the 1300s by King David I. In common with other Fife coastal towns, the arrival of the railway in 1856 stimulated Lower Largo's tourism as visitors flocked to the extensive sandy beaches, depicted in these postcards from 1910 (above) and 1905 (below). The lower one shows Largo Law behind the new town. There was a steamboat from Largo Harbour to Newhaven near Edinburgh during the nineteenth century. The village was designated a conservation area in 1978. *(BD)*

Largo's most famous son is undoubtedly Alexander Selkirk (1676–1721). He went to sea in 1695 and by 1703 was master of the *Cinque Ports*, one of the two ships on a privateering voyage under William Dampier. Off the Juan Fernández Islands near Chile, Selkirk fell out with the captain of his ship and was put ashore at his own request in October 1704 on Más a Tierra Island (now Isla Robinson Crusoe). He lived there alone until he was rescued in February 1709 by another privateering ship, the *Duke*. However, Selkirk was something of a fantasist. He greatly romanticised his adventures and became a dissolute drunk. After marrying two women he escaped to sea again on the English man-of-war *Weymouth* and died horribly of yellow fever in 1721. Many eighteenth-century authors wrote up his exploits, including the essayist Sir Richard Steele and – best known of all – the novelist Daniel Defoe who visited Lower Largo in 1706 and was inspired to write *The Life and Surprising Adventures of Robinson Crusoe*. The statue in the postcard is on a building on the site of the house where Selkirk was born. *(BD)*

The second millennium BC standing stones of Lundie, now within Lundin Ladies Golf Club, are pictured above in 1900. Lundin Links developed as a nineteenth-century resort and suburban dormitory extension of Lower Largo, accommodating holidaymakers. It takes its name from the Lundin family who were granted land here in the twelfth century and built Lundie Tower, a popular subject for a postcard view, like this one from 1907. *(BD)*

The fine beach and sea-front houses at Lundin Links attracted many Edwardian visitors. Golf is still a major attraction. *(BD)*

Leven Road, Lundin Links

5

The East Neuk

Anstruther in 1900 (*BD*)

Elie, Liberty, Williamsburgh and Earlsferry were united as the burgh of Elie and Earlsferry in 1929. Elie's wide harbour and mile-long beach in a curved bay have long been popular with holidaymakers and watersports enthusiasts, as these pictures from 1927 show. To this day, yacht regattas are held in summer. Elie is one of few harbours in Scotland run by a private company for the burgh and its people. *(BD)*

Beyond Ruby Bay – named for the gem stones (mostly garnets) to be found there – Elie Ness bears the ruins of The Lady's Tower, shown here in a postcard from 1900. It was built as a seaside summer house for Janet, Lady Anstruther, an early proponent of the virtues of sea bathing. Elie house, built in 1697 for the Anstruthers, was cursed by a gypsy who predicted that the family would not live there for seven generations and indeed only six generations did. *(BD)*

Elie's name comes from 'Ailie of Ardross', an island which formed part of the natural harbour and was accessible only at low tide. After Elie received its royal charter from James VI in 1589 it became a centre for fishing, boatbuilding, weaving and commerce in general. *(ND)*

The main street in Elie is largely unchanged, although the shops are even more tourist-focused than ever. The Green is remarkable for its shape, which is that of a boat. *(ND)*

Earlsferry is an old village and port from which ferries sailed to North Berwick, Leith and other places in Lothian. The name refers to Macduff, Thane (Earl) of Fife in the eleventh century who, fleeing the clutches of Macbeth, took refuge in a cave near Kincraig Point until a local fisherman could ferry him to Dunbar. An old chapel, now ruined, gave shelter for pilgrims travelling to and from St Andrews. Cadgers Road, which today crosses the golf course, was used by carriers or 'cadgers' to take fresh fish to the royal palace at Falkland. In the twentieth century Earlsferry developed as a popular holiday and residential resort, as this charming 1911 postcard of a sunset shows. *(BD)*

The Isle of May, the largest of the islands in the Firth of Forth, lies 5 miles off the East Neuk coast. Over a mile square, it was designated a national nature reserve in 1956 because of its migrant seabird and grey seal colonies. As this undated postcard shows, the Isle has long been a popular tourist destination. Short trips are now possible from Crail and bird-watchers can arrange longer stays. *(BD)*

St Monans Church, 1905. St Monans (or St Monance) is an old fishing community, close knit to this day in defiance of the struggle to live on the windy seashore. Originally called Inverin, the village took its present name from St Monan who may have lived in a cave near the church and may have been killed by invading pirates. More likely, it was founded in the ninth century by Irish clergy who fled to Scotland, bringing the relics of St Moineinn with them. The present church, built in the 1360s on the instructions of David II in gratitude for his rescue after his ship was wrecked in the Forth, replaced the earlier chapel on the site. One of the oldest churches still in use in Scotland, it was renovated in 1828 although much of the original stonework is visible. The main industries at St Monans were fishing, salt-panning and coalmining but in the twentieth century the trend has been towards tourism and boatbuilding, plus fish-smoking and other new industries on the Netherton Estate. *(BD)*

Pittenweem is the centre of the fishing industry in Fife. White fish was once the main catch of the fleet but today it provides langoustine and other *fruits de mer* for restaurants in France and Spain. The sturdy stone harbour, which replaced the earlier Boat Haven, was built around 1600. Pittenweem has a thriving fish market and an annual festival each August. A feature of this is that many local artists open up their homes as galleries for the week. Many of the old, picturesque houses have been restored by the National Trust for Scotland, including The Gyles, pictured here in 1905. *(BD)*

While the fishing industry naturally developed around Pittenweem's harbour, the commerce centered around Market Square and the High Street at the top of the steep Wynds ascending from the shore. Here the parish church and tolbooth were built in 1588, with council chambers on the first floor of the tower and dungeons below. Pittenweem had a reputation for zealous witch hunting and many a victim was imprisoned here before being executed – the last was Janet Cornfoot in 1704. *(ND)*

The name Pittenweem may derive from Pictish words meaning 'place of the cave'. There is evidence of a Pictish settlement, but St Fillan's Cave in Cove Wynd is believed to have been the saint's retreat in the seventh century. It was a place of worship for centuries and is also said to have been used by local smugglers who used a staircase leading from the cave to the Priory Gardens above. The cave, restored in 1935 as this contemporary postcard shows, is still open to visitors. Inside is the Saint's Well and an altar where St Fillan wrote, helped by a luminous glow from his left arm! *(BD)*

Anstruther gained its royal charter in 1587. In its heyday it was one of the busiest ports in the East Neuk of Fife. The postcard above shows the view from the north and the new outer harbour wall, built in 1868 by Robert Louis Stevenson's father. The young author-to-be stayed in Cunzie House nearby and Anstruther clearly made a great impression on him, as can be seen in his later seafaring adventure tales. The postcard below shows the West Sands. Both images date from *c*. 1910. *(BD)*

Anstruther has weathered the decline of the fishing industry by developing its tourism potential, which is obvious in this post-war picture of Billowness. More recently it has consolidated this with two great attractions – the Scottish Fisheries Museum and, reputedly, the best fish and chip shop in the British Isles. *(BD)*

The parish church in Anstruther West, 1930s. The church sits at the mouth of the Dreel Burn which splits Anstruther Easter from Anstruther Wester. King James V is said to have been carried across the river when it was in spate on the back of an old beggar woman during one of his peripatetic and anonymous 'meet the people' tours. She received the king's purse as a reward! *(BD)*

Thomas Chalmers was born in 1780 in this cottage off Anstruther's High Street, which was photographed in about 1900. He was instrumental in forming the Free Church of Scotland. Chalmers went to St Andrews University at the age of eleven and at twenty-three was both minister at Kilmeny and a science lecturer at the university. In 1815 he became minister of the Tron church in Glasgow (now a theatre) where he organised poor relief, established parochial schools and district churches, wrote and preached prolifically and became justly famous. In 1823 he took the chair of moral philosophy at St Andrews University and in 1838 he was appointed professor of theology at Edinburgh. Between times he became Moderator of the General Assembly of the Church of Scotland and in 1834 proposed the Veto Act which gave parishes the right to reject a minister chosen by the local wealthy patron. This led to a crisis in the Church of Scotland and the Disruption of 1843 in which Chalmers led a third of the ministery (almost 500 men) out of the established church and away from their manses and livings to create the Free Church of Scotland. Every church member paid one penny a week and within two years 500 churches had been built. Chalmers' organisational skills were such that by the time he died in 1847 almost every presbytery in Scotland had a minister of the new Free Church alongside the established Kirk, particularly in the Highlands. Chalmers is also remembered in Chalmers' Lighthouse in Anstruther harbour, seen here just before the Second World War. *(BD)*

Crail is the oldest burgh in the East Neuk. It became a royal burgh in the twelfth century and received an unusual and controversial charter in 1310 from Robert the Bruce allowing it to hold markets on Sundays. These were held in the Marketgait where the seventeenth-century Mercat Cross stands and were once among the largest in Europe. The sixteenth-century tolbooth tower with its rare Dutch roof has a fish-shaped weathervane depicting a Crail capon – a split and sun-dried haddock, a local delicacy. The tolbooth housed the old council chamber, courtroom and prison. *(BD)*

In Marketgait is Crail parish church, seen here in the 1920s. A church has stood on this site since the twelfth century. John Knox preached here in 1559. Outside the church is the 'Devil's Blue Stane', a rock hurled by the Devil when the church was being built. It has a rounded indentation known as the Devil's thumbprint. Sharpening a weapon on the thumbprint is said to guarantee victory. The church grounds include a 'mort house' – a fortified building for storing corpses from the days when body snatchers were common. *(BD)*

The Bow Butts, Crail, 1913. This postcard of the popular beauty spot bears the stark message 'Sat. mng. Wet. Very.' *(BD)*

Crail still caters for tourists and fishermen; it retains its charm. *(ND)*

ACKNOWLEDGEMENTS

Any book is an amalgam of influences. This one owes a lot to the following: Don Swanson (who never gets the real credit due to him) was ever his usual cheerful and helpful self, contributing many rare and valuable photographs; John Sinclair (Scotland's second funniest man) gave of the very pictures from his mum's living room when she wasn't looking; Mr & Mrs Derry Sinclair were very happy to contribute; Louisa, Jeanette and Mo made sure that when inspiration was in short supply, there was beverage enow to make up for it; Nick and Gilly used the opportunity of a few missing photos to redecorate the Harbour Bar; Ian B. Anderson provided much useful information, particularly on the harbour, Ravenscraig and Dysart; the staff at Kirkcaldy Library, especially Janet Klak, Audrey Cunningham and Sheila Brown, were helpfulness itself; my parents provided many valuable historical insights, as well as the usual encouragement; Natasha's unique perspective brought a new shape to the project; Jamie and Anna largely gave me the space and time to do it; and Caroline Parkinson would have got more involved if she hadn't escaped to America. Special thanks are due to Cllr Jock Cameron for information on Dysart and other matters; Andrew Molson, Kevin O'Kane and Bill Mair of Fife Council were a great help and source of photographs; Nick Brand, Iain Somerville and Brian Baxter helped greatly with Burntisland. Thanks also to Carolyne Smith, Tommy Manson and Snowy (who knows everything).

PICTURE CREDITS

Postcards and photographs used in this book attributed BD are taken from Bruce Durie's private collection. They have been given to Kirkcaldy Central Library and are available for public view.

BB	Brian Baxter
CP	Caroline Parkinson
DS	Don Swanson
FC	Fife Council
JS	John Sinclair
KYL	Kirkcaldy Libraries
NB	Nick Brand
ND	Nataliya Durie
NGB	Nick & Gilly Bromfield

All other images are public domain and/or copyright-free. The greatest care has been taken to ensure that all copyrights are acknowledged and rights acquired to use them in this book

INDEX